Crime in the Library

Crime in the Library

A Study of Patterns, Impact, and Security

Alan Jay Lincoln

R. R. BOWKER COMPANY
New York and London, 1984

Library Journal articles (individually credited throughout the text) are reprinted from *Library Journal*. Published by R. R. Bowker Co. Copyright © by Reed Publishing (USA) Inc.

P. 1, "Addicts and Vandals Troubling City Libraries," by Barbara Basler, July 11, 1981; copyright © 1981 by The New York Times Company.

Pp. 1–2, "The editors' page one: 'We are all in the gutter,'" reprinted by permission of the American Library Association from *American Libraries* 14 (5): 260 (May 1983); copyright © 1983 by the American Library Association.

Pp. 56–58, "In New York: Reading Between the Lions," Copyright © 1979 Time Inc. All rights reserved. Reprinted by permission from Time.

P. 61, "Knife-wielding youth slays public library staff member," reprinted by permission of the American Library Association from *American Libraries* 14 (4): 174 (Apr. 1983); copyright © 1983 by the American Library Association.

P. 63, "U of Fla. library director shot by former employee," reprinted by permission of the American Library Association from *American Libraries* 14 (6): 334 (June 1983); copyright © 1983 by the American Library Association.

P. 154, Cantwell, B., "Director says rules a key for calm library." Lawrence *Eagle-Tribune*, March 27, 1983.

Published by R. R. Bowker Company,
a division of Reed Publishing (USA) Inc.
Copyright © 1984 by Reed Publishing (USA) Inc.
All rights reserved
Printed and bound in the United States of America

Except as permitted under the Copyright Act of 1976,
no part of this publication may be reproduced or transmitted
in any form or by any means, stored in any information storage
and retrieval system, without prior written permission of
R. R. Bowker Company, 245 West 17 Street, New York, NY 10011.

Library of Congress Cataloging in Publication Data

Lincoln, Alan Jay.
　Crime in the library.
　　Includes index.
　　1. Libraries—Security measures.　2. Crime and criminals. I. Title.
Z679.6.L56 1984　　　025.8′2　　　83-22288
ISBN 0-8352-1863-5

Design by Jennie Nichols/Levavi & Levavi

For Carol

CONTENTS

PREFACE ix

CHAPTER 1 CRIME AND DISRUPTION IN
PUBLIC PLACES 1
What Is a Public Place? 2
Measuring Crime 4
Crime Patterns in the United States 8
What Is a Crime? 19
Causes of Crime 21

CHAPTER 2 CRIME STUDIES 27
Commercial Crime 27
In Schools 29
In Religious Institutions 30
Public Transportation 31
Recreational Areas 32
In Libraries 33

CHAPTER 3 LIBRARY CRIME RESEARCH PROJECT 66
Procedure and Sample 66
Crime Patterns 71
High- and Low-Crime Libraries 80
Regional Patterns 83
Personal Victimization 85
Trends Over Time 86

CHAPTER 4 THE IMPACT OF CRIME   88
        National Findings: Direct Costs   91
        National Findings: Indirect Costs   97

CHAPTER 5 LIBRARY AND COMMUNITY FACTORS
        AFFECTING CRIME   109
        State-Level Data   110
        Library Characteristics   112
        Community Characteristics   121

CHAPTER 6 PROTECTING THE LIBRARY   127
        Current Findings   127
        Dealing with Major Problems   130
        Crime Prevention Programs   136
        Low-Cost Protection   143
        Designing a Security Program   155

APPENDIX: LIBRARY CRIME RESEARCH PROJECT   163
        A. Survey Questionnaire   163
        B. State Data Acquisition Form   171

INDEX   173

PREFACE

The public image of the library is generally that of a quiet, comfortable, inviting place, a place where people read and study, and certainly a place where people and their belongings should be safe. But recent trends that are showing up in many communities suggest that this may not always be true. The library, like other public institutions, is being confronted with the problems of contemporary American society. And, unfortunately, one of those problems is a relatively high and persistent crime rate.

In the following chapters we examine the patterns of crime that affect libraries. *Crime in the Library* is one of the first books to explore the full range of behavior problems that touch our libraries. It is concerned not only with the ways in which crime affects libraries, but also with the all-important ways in which the library staff can have an effect on reducing crime.

Although the focus throughout this book is on the library, important material from the fields of criminology, security, and the relatively new area of "victimology" is also examined. Through this interdisciplinary approach, the reader can gain an understanding not only of the problems that affect libraries, but of ways to minimize the effects that these disruptive episodes have on the staff, patrons, and the institution itself.

Chapter 1 presents a framework for the study of crime in the library and other public places. In addition, up-to-date information on crime trends in the United States, techniques for measuring crime, and the causes of crime is included.

Chapter 2 reviews relevant literature in library science as well as the social sciences. The problems faced by libraries and other public institutions are examined, as well as the steps being taken to solve them.

Chapter 3 looks at the findings of a major study of library crime, describing national and regional library crime patterns based on surveys conducted in all 50 states. These include data on 18 different types of crime and disruption. The conceptual overview results in a typology of crime and disruption that focuses on four major types of problems:

1. Crimes of theft—problems of book theft, material theft, equipment theft, theft of personal property from staff and patron, and so on. Although book thefts are the most common, their impact may not be as great as other thefts on the functioning of the institution.

2. Vandalism. Most libraries, like other public buildings, suffer an assortment of vandalism acts. The wide range of behavior includes vandalism outside and inside the building, to equipment, and to personal property such as cars parked in library lots. Some acts are relatively minor and their impact is quickly absorbed; others including arson may virtually destroy the physical plant.

3. Personal assaults. Although far less common that other crimes, personal assaults are perhaps the most feared crime in the public sector. Fear of possible assault is inconsistent with a comfortable and efficient work setting.

4. Problem patron behavior. Many forms of deviant patron (and staff) behavior are exhibited by a minority of those who use the library. These range from harassment to indecent exposure, to drug use and sales, and a full range of irrational outbursts. Patterns and implications of these behaviors are described.

Chapter 4 on the costs of crime stresses the impact of various crimes on the institution and those involved with it. Once again, data from the national survey are presented to show the varied effects of crime on the safe and efficient functioning of the library. Here is information on direct and indirect crime costs, the ripple effect, and problems related to crime reporting. Important changes in opinion and behavior that often follow victimization or the fear of victimization are discussed. Survey data relating to budget impact and effects on services are highlighted. Finally, the patterns and costs of various security systems and measures are described.

Chapter 5 begins with a discussion of the risk factors common to many libraries. Additional institutional characteristics such as size, patron use patterns, and location within the community are examined. The way in which various community characteristics affect crime patterns is explored, using original data from the national library crime research project. These include the relationship between city size and crime frequency, the social features of the neighborhood in which the library is located, and the proximity of other public institutions such as schools and police stations.

Many factors that contribute to crime are beyond the control of most library systems. It is not usually feasible to rebuild a facility merely because the neighborhood is no longer an appropriate setting. It is not feasible to provide services only to advantaged adults within the community. It is not feasible to control the growth of population in order to lower crime frequency. However, many conditions *are* within the control of the library staff. In chapter 6, Protecting the Library, we focus on those systems and programs that have been shown to be effective in reducing or preventing crime. Findings are summarized related to the use patterns of 14 different security items in public libraries, followed by an overview of general types of security measures. Recognizing that not all libraries can afford or need sophisticated systems, we describe several low-cost crime prevention programs. The importance of recognizing and assessing local problems is addressed by presenting a working "security checklist," and the chapter ends with suggestions for the development of a comprehensive security program.

Most librarians today recognize the increasing problems brought on by crime and disruption both inside and outside the facility. *Crime in the Library* can aid librarians and staff by broadening their understanding of crime factors and by helping them to recognize what individuals can do in the library setting to reverse the escalating crime rate. And the rate of crime must be reversed if our libraries are to be all they were intended to be to the people who run them and to the patrons they serve.

ACKNOWLEDGMENTS

A project of this size and duration naturally requires the cooperation of many people. In this case I have been very fortunate. Throughout the project I have had the support of my wife, Carol. She has given both her personal support and patience as well as her professional advice as a librarian. My children, Alisa and Debra, have encouraged me to finish the book and have been so understanding when the going was tough. Many of my students in the Criminal Justice Research Seminar at the University of Lowell provided valuable assistance and helped to make this a solid piece of research. There also are literally thousands of librarians from all over the country who took the time to complete our surveys and provide numerous suggestions and comments. To all of you I am grateful.

1 CRIME AND DISRUPTION IN PUBLIC PLACES

Crime is a major problem facing many if not most American cities and towns. The problem affects not only metropolitan areas, but smaller cities and suburban sites as well. What appear to be increasing rates of crime and disruption in public libraries, in addition to the already high crime levels in and against schools and other municipal buildings, are placing added burdens on law enforcement agencies. These burdens are increased in many locations because of cutbacks in local budgets.

The effects of these problems are widespread. Not only are institutions affected by the increased costs of crime, but staff are inconvenienced both professionally and personally. Patrons, too, are involved. Their perceptions about the library as a haven may change, thus affecting their behavior with regard to library use.

Following are two glimpses of what seems to be an increasing part of the library world in the 1980s:

> New York City's librarians are struggling to preserve not only their traditional peace and quiet, but also their very safety as they fend off drug addicts, vandals, thieves, derelicts and teenagers who curse and even threaten the staff. . . . "We've lost the subways and most of the parks and we just can't afford to lose our libraries," said Thomas E. Slade, the assistant police commissioner for legal affairs. "We've got to control these problems before the scale tips."[1]
>
> We are all in the gutter, but some of us are looking at the stars. You bet, Mr. Wilde. We in Libraryland have been gutterbound so long, it seems almost like home. When were we last out of it? Some time in the sixties, one faintly

recalls. It hasn't been easy, Oscar, to keep our eyes on the stars while awash in our own detritus. . . . Yes, we know the gutter well. As a 1982 annual report, a San Francisco branch librarian submitted a daily list of woes, including the following: 2/22—Flasher thrown out. 5/12—Crazy smelly threatened librarians with slashing. 8/14—Copy machine robbed. 12/27—Lady with dog caused mess in Children's Room. . . . And yet . . . miraculously, some of us are still looking at the stars. Two British librarians noticed it. Reporting recently after an exchange visit, they cited "American librarians' optimism, enthusiasm, willingness to embrace technology, and preparedness to overcome problems." . . . But whatever the number and our circumstances, it is spring, and time to look up again. If the gutter has us down, we need only think of Mabel, a clerk in the St. Johns–Apache County Library (Arizona), and her predecessor there. Twenty years ago, Mabel's predecessor fell sick and offered these dying words to her daughter: "Tell Mabel to keep the library open."[2]

"Keep the library open"—not always as easy these days as it sounds. There is an interesting contrast in the above remarks concerning "life in the gutter." As some libraries begin to slip in that direction, some librarians may be tempted to give up, to throw in the towel. Yet the problems faced by many libraries today are not insurmountable. In fact, compared with other public institutions, problems of disruption may be less serious in the library. This does not mean that trouble can or should be ignored in the hope that it will go away. Rather, local problems should be attended to—promptly, fairly, and firmly.

Problems in the library eventually may affect the community as a whole. Important attitudes about crime and safety may be influenced by what happens in those institutions that are supposed to be safe places to visit. Many opinion leaders use the public library. What happens to them and what they see in and around the facility may have important consequences on the perceptions of the quality of life in the community.

WHAT IS A PUBLIC PLACE?

The term *public place* is not as simple to define as it appears. To gain a better understanding of the problems of crime in public places, we use two sets of criteria to classify a location. First, let us consider the ownership of the location. The area in question may be either privately or publicly owned. This is the common use of the term *public*. On the public side we find settings such as municipal parks, museums, libraries, police departments, fire stations, city hospitals, and so on. Although these places share the trait of public ownership, they differ in the way that they treat the public. This brings us to the second criterion, whether access by the public is encouraged or discouraged (see Figure 1). Libraries, mass transit facilities,

	Public Ownership	Private Ownership
Public Access Encouraged	Parks Museums Libraries Zoos Mass transit Schools	Movies Shopping centers Churches Restaurants Recreational areas
Public Access Restricted	Military Police Fire Health facilities Government buildings	Homes Offices Country clubs Industries Factories

■ Figure 1 An overview of public and private places.

parks, and museums encourage access by the public. In fact, their very existence usually is dependent on public use and support. Police departments, fire stations, and government agencies are publicly owned, but the public is, generally speaking, not particularly welcome. Actually, these institutions function more efficiently when access to the public is limited.

To a lesser degree, public schools are moving into that category. Although they are open to members of the community, there are restrictions on access during and after school hours. This was not always the case, nor do all schools restrict access even today. However, as crime in schools increased, especially since the 1960s, many systems instituted visitor control programs.

One of the critical problems facing many urban libraries is the degree to which they can remain in the first category of open access without being forced to move toward the second category of limited access. A compromise used in many public institutions is to separate "front stage" from "back stage" more distinctly. The areas in which the public is allowed become clearly marked as do the areas from which the public is excluded. Police departments and city hospitals have lobbies and waiting rooms to accommodate the public in a controlled setting, but the "real workings" of the facilities are restricted from the casual visitor. When libraries use closed stacks, they are making similar distinctions.

What about the "private" side of Figure 1? Clearly, the public is not restricted from all the locations described here. Once again, we must consider both criteria. Privately owned settings often encourage as much or even more access than do the institutions described as public. Movies, theaters, sports stadiums, and other entertainment facilities must have easy access by the paying public. Shopping centers and other retail establishments also rely on the flow of public traffic. The open door policy of religious institutions was noteworthy until fairly recently. But crime and the fear of crime have caused many churches and synagogues to institute a more restricted access policy. The clearest example of privately held property from which the public generally is excluded is "home." Families go to extraordinary lengths to restrict public access to their own homes. Occasionally these restrictions serve to imprison the inhabitants as well.

> As a result, old people—black and white alike—live like prisoners in the decaying sections of the city. One woman was even afraid to put out her trash: she stuffed it in plastic bags, which she stored in a spare room. When one room would fill up, she would seal it off and start filling up another. At times she lived on candy bars, tossing coins out of a window to children who would go to the store for her.[3]

Many businesses and offices also restrict public access. In fact, most noncommercial establishments have some type of visitor control policy today.

If viewed as a continuum from open access to closed, the public library falls very close to the open end. And this ease of access is one of the risk factors that facilitates crime. (Chapter 5 deals with this and other risk factors in detail; Chapter 6 discusses various prevention programs.) Academic and special libraries typically have more control over entry, but even these often are located within larger institutions that serve the public. The dilemma, then, is how best to meet the needs of the patron and still maintain necessary safety and security measures.

MEASURING CRIME

To fully understand crime patterns and how to reduce crime in public settings, we must first have some familiarity with how social scientists measure crime. Accurately assessing the incidence and pattern of crime is essential before developing programs to deter, control, or modify the effects of crime.

Measuring criminal behavior is not as simple as, say, measuring births and deaths or marriages. Most social problems, including crime, not surprisingly, tend to be hidden by the participants. Thus, criminal behavior is not always apparent to the concerned observer. However, a variety of techniques are used by scientists in the social sciences and in criminal justice to measure and determine the patterns of crime. Whether one technique or another is chosen depends in part on the needs and resources of the researcher. Four distinct ways of measuring crime are: (1) reported crime statistics, (2) victimization surveys, (3) offender surveys, and (4) existing agency records. The strengths and weaknesses of each are explained briefly in the following pages. Conceivably, a program to assess and then reduce crime in libraries or other public settings could utilize any one or a combination of these methods.

Reported Crime

One of the most common ways of assessing crime in a state or community is to examine data on known crimes in the *Uniform Crime Reports* (*U.C.R.*), published by the Federal Bureau of Investigation. These reports contain valuable information on crime reported to police. The key here is that the crimes must have been *reported* to a law enforcement agency in order to be included in the reports.

The process begins at the local level where all crimes known to the police are recorded. Crimes "known to the police" include those reported to them and those of which they have firsthand knowledge. Typically, these reports are tabulated on a monthly basis and reported to a state-level collection agency. The state agencies in turn compile their reports for the Department of Justice. The full report, the *Uniform Crime Reports,* is issued annually. Over 15,000 agencies feed information into this final report. The *U.C.R.* is one of the best sources of information on officially known crimes. National, regional, state, and some local level data are available on the number, rate, type, and patterns of crime. The major limitation is that only crimes known to the police are included. If an individual does not know that a crime has been committed or chooses not to report it, that information is never tabulated. The same is true of institutions. Many administrators working in public facilities such as schools and libraries apparently often choose not to report crimes to police.

Victimization Surveys

In part due to the reluctance of many victims or observers to report crimes to law enforcement agencies, social scientists have developed additional ways to measure crime, such as the victimization survey. Basically, a victimization survey solicits information directly from those who are likely to be victims of crimes. The victims of crime can be rich sources of information about the amount of and circumstances surrounding crime.

These surveys can be conducted using individuals or an institution as the unit of analysis. For example, large-scale interviews of a national sample of individuals have shown that the actual crime rates tend to be higher than those reported in the *U.C.R.* Similarly, surveys of schools have been conducted to determine the pattern of institutional victimization. In these surveys, the individuals working or in other ways involved with the agencies can be studied as well. (In later chapters, data from a national survey of library crime patterns are described. These data were obtained using a victimization survey specifically designed for this book.)

Among the advantages of the victim survey is the ability to measure crimes that were not reported to any official agency. In this way, a more accurate assessment of actual crime patterns can be shown, and a great deal can be learned about the circumstances surrounding various crime episodes. Also, the cost of victimization surveys tends to be within the limits of many institutions. This is true particularly when surveys are either mailed or distributed to the respondents. Advances in the use of telephone surveys have reduced the cost even further. Finally, the response rate from these surveys can be quite high, thereby facilitating an accurate estimate of the crime problem.

There are, of course, some difficulties with victimization surveys. First, not all kinds of crime can be measured in this way. Basically, a victim must be aware of his or her victimization in order to respond. If, for example, an administrator does not know that several rare books have been stolen, there will be no way of describing the episode. Similarly, there are many victimless crimes that cannot be reported. Crimes that occur without a victim or with the victim's actual consent—drugs, illicit sexual behavior, illegal gambling—will not be reported in many cases. And depending on the time frame, there may be some problem with recall of criminal events. Generally, asking about happenings more than a year old can be problematic at best. However, institutions often have some type of record that can extend the period of recall. Maintenance reports and work orders for repairs may provide good information about vandalism and other acts of destruction. Finally, the use of a large-scale victimization survey may be prohibitive in cost if personal interviews are conducted by trained interviewers.

Offender Surveys

If we can obtain accurate information about crime from victims and observers, can we also make use of the information provided by the offenders themselves? In some cases, studies focusing on offenders can be very useful. If, for example, you are interested in why people steal books or why they deface resource materials, you might simply ask a sampling of patrons. Of course, there are readily apparent drawbacks to this direct approach. Information about victimless crimes may indeed be obtained from offenders and motivations of offenders may be examined, but there is also the very real possibility that informants will not give the researcher complete information about their criminal activities. In addition, among some segments of the population, notably juveniles, there may be the opposite problem—a tendency to exaggerate one's criminality as a way of raising self-esteem or receiving peer approval. Careful questioning can, however, avoid many of these problems.

A failure to give full disclosure of one's actions is most likely to occur when the person is being asked about serious crimes. Criminologists have learned from various offender surveys that rather ordinary people often do extraordinary things. In fact, studies show that many juveniles and adults have done things that, if known to police, could have resulted in legal proceedings. Librarians often suspect that it is their "good" patrons who are likely to steal books. The motives and techniques of offenders often can be uncovered by the use of offender surveys. This is true particularly when interviews are used in conjunction with the research. This information can be invaluable to administrators of public institutions.

The development of an offender survey is similar to that of a victimization survey. Proper care must be taken in the selection of the sample, the design of the survey instrument, and the administration of the actual questions. When using either a victimization survey or an offender survey, it is important to obtain a representative sample and return.

The response rate for surveys of any kind—whether they deal with crime, patron needs, or anything else—can be affected by several factors. One is the ease of completion. Generally, surveys should be clear and concise. The sponsorship of the study also can be a factor. Agencies or sponsors that are seen by respondents as important, legitimate, and worthwhile generally receive higher returns than others. When dealing with sensitive issues such as crime, maintaining the anonymity of the respondent is not only important, but in some cases of government-funded research is required by law. This anonymity also facilitates more accurate disclosure and higher returns. Inducements to respond can be quite important, too. Even so simple an inducement as providing a self-addressed stamped envelope has proved helpful in boosting the return rate.

Existing Agency Records

The fourth technique for obtaining information about crime is to use existing records. Whenever anyone becomes involved with the criminal justice system of the United States, he or she usually triggers a massive record-keeping procedure. These records begin at the early stages of police contact and continue throughout contact with the system. Records kept by police, courts, social agencies, correctional facilities, juvenile agencies, and so on could be useful and inexpensive sources of information related to an individual library's crime problem. However, since each different set of records tends to focus on a somewhat different aspect of the crime, care is needed when attempting to apply this information to a specific local problem.

The most common drawback to this technique is legitimate access to the information. In some cases data are available to the public, but not always. Almost all information regarding specific juvenile cases is restricted. Information about the general problem of juvenile crime may be available, but not data about specific individuals or cases. All information collected by specific agencies within the criminal justice system reflects the official response of that agency to the crime problem. That is, court records reflect the patterns of court response, and prison records reflect the response of prisons.

At each stage, from police investigation to arrest, trial, conviction, treatment, aftercare, and so on, there is a trickle effect of suspects dropping out of the system. The further along the stage, the more the records reflect information about a restricted group of criminals. Studying why jailed criminals steal is not quite the same as studying why a nonimprisoned group might steal. Care should be taken to match the study sample to the needs of the institution.

Keep in mind that measuring crime and related problems of disruption is a complex task, with many options available. The choice of one or another depends on the needs of the researcher as well as the available resources. Any one or a combination of several different techniques may prove adequate for obtaining the information needed in a particular instance.

CRIME PATTERNS IN THE UNITED STATES

The usual way to describe crime patterns is to examine the crime rate. Like any other rate, the crime rate is determined by establishing the number of occurrences for a specified unit of the population. For example, we tabulate the number of murders per so many thousand people in a state to ascertain that state's murder rate. When national- or state-level information is being described, the rate is typically for units of 100,000. That is, the number of crimes for every 100,000 people is examined. In this way, crime rates for locations of different populations can be compared. If we used only the absolute number of crimes in a comparison, the more heavily populated states would, of course, have more crimes, but we would not know whether they had more crimes per person (or per 100,000 persons). A library administrator likely would want to know the absolute

TABLE 1

NUMBER AND RATES OF REPORTED CRIMES IN THE UNITED STATES*

	Total Number	Rate/100,000
Violent crime	1,321,906	576.9
Murder and nonnegligent manslaughter	22,516	9.8
Forcible rape	81,536	35.6
Robbery	574,136	250.6
Aggravated assault	643,720	280.9
Property crime	11,968,350	5,223.0
Burglary	3,789,821	1,632.1
Larceny-theft	7,154,541	3,122.3
Motor vehicle theft	1,073,988	468.7
Crime Index total[†]	13,290,256	5,799.9

*For the year 1981.
[†]Total of violent crime and property crime figures.
Adapted from *Crime in the United States*, 1982.

number of thefts in the institution as well as how the crime rate at that particular library compared with similar, smaller, and larger libraries.

Statistics presented each year in the *Uniform Crime Reports* are broken down into two types of crimes. Type I offenses describe the most serious crimes, including murder, aggravated assault, rape, robbery, burglary, larceny-theft, and motor vehicle theft. Starting in 1979, arson was added to this list. Type II crimes are considered less serious and include more than 20 other offenses, such as simple assault, vandalism, fraud, prostitution, some juvenile offenses, drug violations, and so on.

Type I offenses are combined into a crime index, which provides a summary measure of crime rates at the local, state, regional, and national levels.

Table 1 shows rates for Type I offenses in the United States for a given year. Note that the rates for these offenses vary from 9.8 for murder to 3,122 for larceny-theft. Also note that the rate for violent crimes (murder, rape, robbery, aggravated assault) is nearly ten times lower than the rate for property crimes. Yet the public fears violent crimes (which occur far less often) far more than they fear nonviolent crimes. This suggests that reactions to crime are based not only on likelihood of occurrence but on perceived impact as well. The average individual is far more frightened at

TABLE 2

RATES OF OFFENSES KNOWN TO POLICE, BY OFFENSE, UNITED STATES, 1960–1979 (PER 100,000 INHABITANTS)

Year	Crime Index Total	Violent Crime	Property Crime	Murder and Nonnegligent Manslaughter	Forcible Rape	Robbery	Aggravated Assault	Burglary	Larceny-Theft	Motor Vehicle Theft
1960	1,887.2	160.9	1,726.3	5.1	9.6	60.1	86.1	508.6	1,034.7	183.0
1961	1,906.1	158.1	1,747.9	4.8	9.4	58.3	85.7	518.9	1,045.4	183.6
1962	2,019.8	162.3	1,857.5	4.6	9.4	59.7	88.6	535.2	1,124.8	197.4
1963	2,180.3	168.2	2,012.1	4.6	9.4	61.8	92.4	576.4	1,219.1	216.6
1964	2,388.1	190.6	2,197.5	4.9	11.2	68.2	106.2	634.7	1,315.5	247.4
1965	2,449.0	200.2	2,248.8	5.1	12.1	71.7	111.3	662.7	1,329.3	256.8
1966	2,670.8	220.0	2,450.9	5.6	13.2	80.8	120.3	721.0	1,442.9	286.9
1967	2,989.7	253.2	2,736.5	6.2	14.0	102.8	130.2	826.6	1,575.8	334.1
1968	3,370.2	298.4	3,071.8	6.9	15.9	131.8	143.8	932.3	1,746.6	393.0
1969	3,680.0	328.7	3,351.3	7.3	18.5	148.4	154.5	984.1	1,930.9	436.2
1970	3,984.5	363.5	3,621.0	7.9	18.7	172.1	164.8	1,084.9	2,079.3	456.8
1971	4,164.7	396.0	3,766.8	8.6	20.5	188.0	178.8	1,163.5	2,145.5	459.8
1972	3,961.4	401.0	3,560.4	9.0	22.5	180.7	188.8	1,140.8	1,993.6	426.1
1973	4,154.4	417.4	3,737.0	9.4	24.5	183.1	200.5	1,222.5	2,071.9	442.6
1974	4,850.4	461.1	4,389.3	9.8	26.2	209.3	215.8	1,437.7	2,489.5	462.2
1975	5,281.7	481.5	4,800.2	9.6	26.3	218.2	227.4	1,525.9	2,804.8	469.4
1976	5,266.4	459.8	4,806.8	8.8	26.4	195.8	228.7	1,439.4	2,921.3	446.1
1977	5,055.1	466.6	4,588.4	8.8	29.1	187.1	241.5	1,410.9	2,729.9	447.6
1978	5,109.3	486.9	4,622.4	9.0	30.8	191.3	255.9	1,423.7	2,743.9	454.7
1979	5,521.5	535.5	4,986.0	9.7	34.5	212.1	279.1	1,499.1	2,988.4	498.5

Adapted from *Crime in the United States*, 1975, 1980.

the prospect, however remote, of physical assault than of having his or her car stolen. (Chapter 4 examines the actual impact of crime on the library in more detail.)

How do the rates in Table 1 compare with crime rates at other times in U.S. history? Basically, crime rates have shown a steady increase in recent decades. There have been several leveling-off periods and even an occasional decline, but the overall trend has been upward.

As shown in Table 2, some crimes have increased dramatically within a relatively short time. Reported violent crimes went up from a rate of 161 in 1960 to 536 in 1979 to 581 in 1980 (not shown in Table 2)—a more than threefold increase. The increase in property crime was not quite as steep. The 1960 rate was 1,726; in 1979 it was 4,986 and in 1980 it had increased to 5,319. The slowest rate of increase during this period was for murder, from 5.1 to 10.2.

One of the striking features of the crime pattern in recent U.S. history is the difference between the rates for urban and rural areas. As everyone suspects, urban areas are more likely to have higher crime rates. However, the magnitude of this difference may be surprising. As can be seen in Table 3, the overall crime rate in the largest cities (Group I) is about twice as high as the rate in small cities (Group VI). The difference is even greater for violent crime. In fact, the most extreme discrepancy is for robbery, where there is more than a tenfold difference. Those concerned with safety and security in libraries should be responsive to these basic differences. Crime patterns in public institutions often reflect the patterns in the surrounding community.

There also are some differences in crime trends according to regions of the country. Crime is overall highest in the West, followed by the northeastern, southern, and midwestern areas. But this pattern breaks down when each type of major crime is considered separately. Murder rates tend to be higher in the southern region of the country; reports of rape occur at the highest rate in the West. Robbery and auto theft affect the northeastern states most; assault and larceny are highest in the West. These differences can be quite large. The rates, of course, take into account population differences, and differences in crime patterns also can be identified at the local level. Sometimes these differences occur between neighboring cities, and other times the differences are most striking when looking at neighborhoods within the same city.

Consistent patterns related to the age of known offenders should be examined by administrators in public institutions. The young in American society tend to be overrepresented in arrests for crime. This, of course, does not mean that all young people should be viewed with suspicion. It does suggest, however, that institutions with a high proportion of youth among users should take sensible security and prevention measures.

TABLE 3

CRIME RATES FOR OFFENSES KNOWN TO POLICE (BY POPULATION GROUP)

Population Group	Crime Index Total	Violent Crime	Property Crime	Murder and Non-negligent Man-slaughter	Forcible Rape	Robbery	Aggravated Assault	Burglary	Larceny-Theft	Motor Vehicle Theft
Total All Agencies (11,933 agencies; pop. 204,526,000)										
Number of offenses known	12,293,334	1,247,416	11,045,918	20,554	75,663	548,038	603,161	3,448,100	6,611,712	986,106
Rate	6,010.6	609.9	5,400.7	10.0	37.0	268.0	294.9	1,685.9	3,232.7	482.1
Total Cities (8,203 cities; pop. 139,688,000)										
Number of offenses known	10,027,636	1,050,522	8,977,114	15,906	59,399	499,682	475,535	2,687,801	5,451,882	837,431
Rate	7,178.6	752.1	6,426.6	11.4	42.5	357.7	340.4	1,924.2	3,902.9	599.5
GROUP I										
250,000 and over (55 cities; pop. 39,657,000)										
Number of offenses known	3,756,001	571,397	3,184,604	9,306	28,942	334,626	198,523	1,050,730	1,710,431	423,443
Rate	9,471.3	1,440.9	8,030.4	23.5	73.0	843.8	500.6	2,649.6	4,313.1	1,067.8
1,000,000 and over (5 cities; pop. 15,995,000)										
Number of offenses known	1,449,851	276,165	1,173,686	4,446	9,948	177,358	84,413	395,620	554,480	223,586
Rate	9,064.5	1,726.6	7,337.9	27.8	62.2	1,108.8	527.8	2,473.4	3,466.6	1,397.9

Population group	Total Crime Index	Violent crime	Property crime	Murder and nonneg. manslaughter	Forcible rape	Robbery	Aggravated assault	Burglary	Larceny-theft	Motor vehicle theft
500,000 to 999,999 (18 cities; pop. 12,147,000)										
Number of offenses known	1,149,623	147,113	1,002,510	2,451	9,262	83,506	51,894	318,491	572,797	111,222
Rate	9,463.9	1,211.1	8,252.8	20.2	76.2	687.4	427.2	2,621.9	4,715.4	915.6
250,000 to 499,999 (32 cities; pop. 11,515,000)										
Number of offenses known	1,156,527	148,119	1,008,408	2,409	9,732	73,762	62,216	336,619	538,154	88,635
Rate	10,044.1	1,286.4	8,757.7	20.9	84.5	640.6	540.3	2,923.4	5,064.5	769.8
GROUP II 100,000 to 249,999 (112 cities; pop. 16,582,000)										
Number of offenses known	1,454,470	137,038	1,317,432	2,174	9,348	57,975	67,541	410,582	808,237	98,613
Rate	8,771.1	826.4	7,944.7	13.1	56.4	349.6	407.3	2,476.0	4,874.0	594.7
GROUP III 50,000 to 99,999 (272 cities; pop. 18,578,000)										
Number of offenses known	1,291,974	108,442	1,183,532	1,382	7,035	42,350	57,675	358,040	721,019	104,473
Rate	6,954.3	583.7	6,370.6	7.4	37.9	228.0	310.4	1,927.2	3,881.0	562.3
Group VI Under 10,000 (5,670 cities; pop. 20,937,000)										
Number of offenses known	996,020	60,918	935,102	836	3,442	11,405	42,235	228,874	656,565	49,663
Rate	4,757.2	291.0	4,466.2	4.0	16.4	54.5	216.0	1,093.1	3,135.9	237.2

Adapted from *Crime in the United States*, 1982.

TABLE 4

ARREST PATTERNS BY AGE FOR INDEX CRIMES AND OTHER OFFENSES

Offense Charged	Total All Ages	Number of Persons Arrested				Percent of Total All Ages				
		Under 15	Under 18	Under 21	Under 25	Under 15	Under 18	Under 21	Under 25
Total	**10,293,575**	**623,018**	**2,035,748**	**3,775,581**	**5,629,422**	**6.1**	**19.8**	**36.7**	**54.7**
Violent crime	464,826	22,106	85,853	163,992	254,581	4.8	18.5	35.3	54.8
Murder and nonnegligent manslaughter	20,432	205	1,858	4,880	8,829	1.0	9.1	23.9	43.2
Forcible rape	30,050	1,193	4,449	9,254	15,593	4.0	14.8	30.8	51.9
Robbery	147,396	10,250	42,214	74,983	104,807	7.0	28.6	50.9	71.1
Aggravated assault	266,948	10,458	37,332	74,875	125,352	3.9	14.0	28.0	47.0
Property crime	1,828,928	260,773	683,655	1,016,968	1,283,965	14.3	37.4	55.6	70.2
Burglary	489,533	71,782	208,650	312,089	387,077	14.7	42.6	63.8	79.1
Larceny-theft	1,197,845	172,064	417,346	620,134	790,649	14.4	34.8	51.8	66.0
Motor vehicle theft	122,188	11,913	49,449	74,087	93,195	9.7	40.5	60.6	76.3
Arson	19,362	5,014	8,210	10,658	13,044	25.9	42.4	55.0	67.4
Crime Index total*	2,293,754	282,879	769,508	1,180,960	1,538,546	12.3	33.5	51.5	67.1
Other assaults	466,359	28,163	79,259	144,487	233,539	6.0	17.0	31.0	50.1
Forgery and counterfeiting	81,429	1,468	8,625	22,308	39,827	1.8	10.6	27.4	48.9
Fraud	272,900	4,639	14,158	40,977	93,846	1.7	5.2	15.0	34.4
Embezzlement	8,170	162	824	2,078	3,633	2.0	10.1	25.4	44.5
Stolen property (buying, receiving, possessing)	122,452	9,074	33,003	58,464	80,859	7.4	27.0	47.7	66.0
Vandalism	228,849	53,908	108,555	146,249	176,826	23.6	47.4	63.9	77.3
Weapons (carrying, possessing, etc.)	170,660	6,294	25,422	52,807	85,106	3.7	14.9	30.9	49.9

*Total of violent crime and property crime figures.
Adapted from *Crime in the United States*, 1982.

Table 4 shows patterns of arrests for persons under 15, 18, 21, and 25 years of age. Note that those under 18 account for 40 percent of all arrests and nearly 20 percent of arrests for violent crimes. Motor vehicle theft, burglary, and arson particularly are likely to result in the arrest of a youth. The proportions of arrests of people under 21 are even higher. Over half of property crime arrests and over one-third of arrests for violent crimes involve these age categories. Data on other offenses show that vandalism is committed primarily by youth.

One additional pattern is important to note. Males are far more likely to be arrested than are females. Studies using data other than arrest records also show that males are far more likely to commit crimes whether or not they are caught and arrested. (However, the rate at which females commit crimes is growing.) Table 5 shows that males account for over 80 percent of the arrests for all major crimes except larceny-theft.

So far we looked at U.S. crime patterns based on crimes known to police. Earlier we noted that the use of a victimization survey has some advantages over the *U.C.R.* Most importantly, victimization surveys provide a more accurate picture of the amount of crime. According to a

TABLE 5

PATTERNS OF ARREST BY SEX*

Offense Charged	Number of Persons Arrested			Percent	
	Total	Male	Female	Male	Female
Total	**10,293,575**	**8,633,408**	**1,660,167**	**83.9**	**16.1**
Violent crime	464,826	417,757	47,069	89.9	10.1
Murder and nonnegligent manslaughter	20,432	17,846	2,586	87.3	12.7
Forcible rape	30,050	29,772	278	99.1	.9
Robbery	147,396	136,816	10,580	92.8	7.2
Aggravated assault	266,948	233,323	33,625	87.4	12.6
Property crime	1,828,928	1,437,084	391,844	78.6	21.4
Burglary	489,533	458,899	30,634	93.7	6.3
Larceny-theft	1,197,845	849,783	348,062	70.9	29.1
Motor vehicle theft	122,188	111,259	10,929	91.1	8.9
Arson	19,362	17,143	2,219	88.5	11.5
Crime Index total[†]	2,293,754	1,854,841	438,913	80.9	19.1

*For the year 1981
[†]Total of violent crime and property crime figures.
Adapted from *Crime in the United States,* 1982.

TABLE 6

VICTIMIZATION RATES FOR PERSONAL AND HOUSEHOLD CRIMES, 1973–1981 (PER 1,000 PERSONS)

Sector & Type of Crime	1973	1974	1975	1976	1977	1978	1979	1980	1981
Personal Sector									
Crimes of violence	32.6	33.0	32.8	32.6	33.9	33.7	34.5	33.3	35.3
Rape	1.0	1.0	0.9	0.8	0.9	1.0	1.1	0.9	1.0
Robbery	6.7	7.2	6.8	6.5	6.2	5.9	6.3	6.6	7.4
Assault	24.9	24.8	25.2	25.3	26.8	26.9	27.2	25.8	27.0
Aggravated assault	10.1	10.4	9.6	9.9	10.0	9.7	9.9	9.3	9.6
Simple assault	14.8	14.4	15.6	15.4	16.8	17.2	17.3	16.5	17.3
Crimes of theft	91.1	95.1	96.0	96.1	97.3	96.8	91.9	83.0	85.1
Personal larceny with contact	3.1	3.1	3.1	2.9	2.7	3.1	2.9	3.0	3.3
Personal larceny without contact	88.0	92.0	92.9	93.2	94.6	93.6	89.0	80.0	81.9
Household Sector									
Household burglary	91.7	93.1	91.7	88.9	88.5	86.0	84.1	84.3	87.9
Household larceny	107.0	123.8	125.4	124.1	123.3	119.9	133.7	126.5	121.0
Motor vehicle theft	19.1	18.8	19.5	16.5	17.0	17.5	17.5	16.7	17.1

Adapted from *Bureau of Justice Statistics Technical Report*, March 1983.

Bureau of Justice Statistics Technical Report (March 1983), the rates of major crimes since the implementation of victimization surveys are substantially higher than those reported in the U.C.R. However, as shown in Table 6, these high rates have remained relatively stable and do not show the rapid increases apparent in the U.C.R. figures. The rates shown in Table 6 are per 1,000 persons; they should be multiplied by 100 to be comparable to the U.C.R. rates. This points out the advantage of asking people about their experiences as victims in addition to examining data on reported crimes. Many administrators, like many private citizens, prefer not to report crimes to police. However, victimization surveys can be designed at a relatively low cost to identify the patterns of crime experienced by library staff and patrons.

Earlier we noted that the young are disproportionately involved in the commission of crimes. Using victimization survey data, we find similar patterns for the young as crime victims. This is true particularly in the case of violent crimes. As seen in Table 7, the peak age of reported victimization for rape and simple assault is between 16 and 19. Other crimes peak before age 24. Notice that the rate declines markedly until the lowest

TABLE 7

ESTIMATED RATE OF PERSONAL VICTIMIZATION, BY AGE OF VICTIM AND TYPE OF VICTIMIZATION, UNITED STATES, 1979 (PER 100,000 PERSONS 12 YEARS OF AGE OR OLDER)

Type of Victimization	Age of Victim						
	12–15	16–19	20–24	25–34	35–49	50–64	65 or Older
Rape and attempted rape	133	316	261	126	55	11	4
Robbery	940	1,037	1,212	602	508	346	247
Robbery with injury	238	383	437	217	147	132	103
Serious assault	110	219	260	129	84	51	30
Minor assault	128	164	177	88	63	81	72
Robbery without injury	387	405	515	227	246	171	85
Attempted robbery without injury	315	249	260	158	115	42	59
Assault	4,266	5,666	5,727	3,656	1,563	674	340
Aggravated assault	1,325	2,081	2,222	1,349	598	231	108
With injury	565	651	779	445	179	80	29
Attempted assault with weapon	760	1,430	1,443	904	419	151	78
Simple assault	2,941	3,585	3,505	2,307	965	443	232
With injury	848	1,002	939	583	243	53	39
Attempted assault without weapon	2,093	2,583	2,566	1,723	722	391	194
Personal larceny with contact	291	270	429	279	210	250	353
Purse snatching	23	84	101	76	35	68	90
Attempted purse snatching	0	8	0	15	21	47	74
Pocket picking	268	177	329	189	154	135	190
Personal larceny without contact	13,898	14,343	14,406	10,491	7,866	5,041	1,811

Adapted from *Sourcebook of Criminal Justice Statistics*, 1981.

TABLE 8

ESTIMATED RATE OF PERSONAL VICTIMIZATION, BY SEX OF VICTIM AND TYPE OF VICTIMIZATION, UNITED STATES, 1979 (PER 100,000 PERSONS 12 YEARS OF AGE OR OLDER)

	Sex of Victim	
Type of Victimization	Male	Female
Base	85,327,511	92,915,494
Rape and attempted rape	24	184
Robbery	875	397
Robbery with injury	288	145
Serious assault	187	47
Minor assault	101	98
Robbery without injury	358	178
Attempted robbery without injury	229	74
Assault	3,650	1,864
Aggravated assault	1,491	534
With injury	487	198
Attempted assault with weapon	1,004	336
Simple assault	2,159	1,329
With injury	510	388
Attempted assault without weapon	1,648	942
Personal larceny with contact	263	308
Purse snatching	0	129
Attempted purse snatching	0	50
Pocket picking	263	129
Personal larceny without contact	9,661	8,199

Adapted from *Sourcebook of Criminal Justice Statistics,* 1981.

likelihood of becoming a victim is for the elderly. However, even though the elderly are statistically the least likely to be victimized, the impact of each act of victimization can be most devastating for this age group.

Males account for the vast majority of arrests. Are they also most likely to be victims? Except for rape and purse snatching, two crimes at opposite ends of a severity continuum, men are more likely to be victimized than are women. Table 8 shows that the personal larceny rates are similar for men and women, but robbery and assault victims are more likely to be males. Once again, we cannot equate the likelihood of being a victim with the impact of victimization. Impact depends on both the characteristics of the victim and the nature of the crime. Subsequent treatment of the risk factors within the library will examine the implications of these crime data for the security of the library.

WHAT IS A CRIME?

A wide range of behavior occurs in libraries and other public places. Most people would easily recognize some specific behaviors as a crime. Other actions might be regarded as criminal by some people but not by others.

The perception of crime may be subjective, but the legal definition of crime is specific. That is, there may be a difference between what an observer calls a crime and what really, according to law, *is* a crime. This discrepancy can manifest itself in two ways. First, a person may break the law because he or she is unaware that a certain action is regarded as criminal. Second, a person may commit an act that actually is a crime, but it may not be defined as illegal by others; for example, stolen books may be defined as long overdue. This is an important distinction when trying to reduce the incidence of crime in libraries. People often act on the basis of their beliefs. Patrons who would not consider breaking the law may do so unwittingly; others who are aware of a specific legal code may violate it by choice. The solutions to these instances are different. Education and information may "reform" the first patron, but may have no effect on the second. Increasing the penalties or the likelihood of apprehension may be a fruitful course for the willing offender, but unnecessary to deal with the unintentional one.

What exactly is a crime? There are many definitions used by legal scholars and social scientists; a quite useful one is suggested by Tappan: "Crime is an intentional act or omission in violation of criminal law (statutory and case law), committed without defense or justification, and sanctioned by the state as a felony or misdemeanor."[4] What exactly does that mean? First, there must be some intent to do something that is prohibited. It does not matter if the offender meant to do one thing but did something else by mistake. For example, a person who burns down a building for insurance money (committing arson) and unintentionally kills a tenant may also be charged with murder in some degree. Normally, if there is general intent to commit a prohibited act, then resulting consequences also become crimes. Another important point is that for a crime to occur, there must be actual behavior or a failure to take action when it is required. Failure to act may be refusal to file tax forms, register a car, or return books. To be a crime, the behavior or failure to act must violate an existing criminal law. If the act is not prohibited by law, it is not a crime.

It should also be noted that situations occur in which acts that are usually prohibited become acceptable behavior in the eyes of the law. These situations fall into the category of defensible or justifiable acts. If you defend yourself against serious physical assault, and your attacker is killed in the process, you will not generally be charged with murder. Recently, several states added or modified existing laws giving homeowners greater flexibility in the use of deadly force to protect themselves from perceived danger. The key point is that the law must specify what is considered justifiable. The decision is not left entirely to the individual.

Regardless of the statutes in existence at a particular time, the definition of laws may change. What is illegal today could very well be legitimate at another time or in another place, and vice versa. Laws are socially influenced. They respond to the needs of society—particularly to the pressure groups within society. The use of the legislative process can be beneficial in helping public institutions deal with some of their problems concerning crime and disruption.

In contrast to law is social deviance. Many actions that are considered unacceptable by the general public are not illegal but deviant. Most behavior falls within the limits of what is considered normative or acceptable. At the same time, each of us has a set of standards that we use to determine whether behavior is appropriate. Whenever the behavior in question, our own or someone else's, is outside that range of acceptability, it is considered deviant. The range of behavior that we will tolerate varies in several ways. We may be more tolerant of the behavior of some people than of others. The crying of a baby is generally tolerated far more than that of an adolescent. The aggressiveness of young males has usually been more accepted than that of young females, although this may be an example of how tolerance can change across time.

Whether actions are considered acceptable also depends on the setting. Behavior that is considered appropriate in one's own home may be perceived as deviant if demonstrated in the school or library. Since deviance is a social definition with individual differences, it is not surprising that people disagree on the range of appropriate behavior. Much disruptive but noncriminal behavior that affects libraries may be a problem of different standards being used by different people. In some of these cases, a careful explanation of what is expected and tolerated may be sufficient to alter the actions. However, in many other cases the behavior is occurring specifically *because* it is known to be offensive to the observer. Defining the limits of tolerable action will have little effect on such offenders.

There is another important point to note about the definition of law and illegal behavior. Some actions that are clearly in violation of law, such as stealing books, are often tolerated by the public. Other examples include "a little cheating" on the income tax, some underage drinking, "rolling" stops at stop signs, and so on. Many libraries face problems because the public or law enforcement agencies fail to take their problems seriously. Occasional book theft is ignored, or at least not regarded as serious, and initiating prosecution is difficult. At times the problem rests with the professionals in the library. If they do not define such behavior as a crime, they and others around them are less likely to take effective action. This can lead to a more widespread problem of pluralistic ignorance. Other professionals may be having similar or even more serious problems, but they too are keeping such information to themselves. This occurs frequently with personnel who have embarrassing or shocking experiences. Such encounters as indecent exposure and verbal harassment often are kept private. Providing a nonthreatening mechanism to encourage staff to report these episodes and to define them appropriately would be a valuable resource.

CAUSES OF CRIME

A major goal of social and behavioral sciences is to uncover the causes of human behavior—a complex but intriguing problem. Many criminologists devote entire careers to searching for clues and developing theories concerning the causes of crime and delinquency. Attempts to reduce or prevent crime are facilitated by an understanding of possible causes, and many organizational methods for examining the causes of crime do exist. Regardless of which framework is selected as most useful, several guidelines are appropriate. Haskell and Yablonsky suggest the following issues as guides for judging the validity of theories about crime and delinquency:[5]

1. A relationship of factors is not necessarily a causal relationship.
2. No single theory explains all crime and delinquency.
3. Primary and secondary causes should not be confused.
4. One cannot logically isolate one single cause of crime or delinquency; causation is a multifactored condition.

Haskell and Yablonsky also suggest two broad categories of crime theory. The first places emphasis on the individual; the second puts emphasis on the group and/or society. Although there certainly are more complicated organizational schemes, this basic dichotomy is good. Most theories thought of as useful explanations for the different types of crime do indeed emphasize either the individual or the society. The contrast becomes even more useful if we recognize that most individuals are constantly involved in social interaction. Furthermore, different people react in different ways to the world around them. People are both individual and social creations. One of the difficulties in making accurate predictions about human behavior is that we do not all perceive and respond to things in the same way. For example, the effect of living in a high crime neighborhood is not the same for all its residents. We need both social and individual perspectives to understand crime.

Emphasis on the Individual

Many early theories of crime attempted to isolate particular traits that would identify an individual as a criminal or potential criminal. Any plan that gave easy clues about who committed crimes was considered valuable. Those criteria would be useful today if such a theory actually was accurate. Unfortunately most attempts failed, but not before the impact of such early theories was made on legislation and practice. One early (and still discussed) suggestion was that criminals were "born that way"; that some inherent difference between criminals and noncriminals exists. Cesare Lombroso (1836–1909), an Italian physician, suggested that criminals were born with physical stigmata and were "throwbacks" to primitive humans. He later modified this theory to include more social factors in the explanation of crime.

More recently, an emphasis on a scientifically measured body type became the focus of possible links to crime. Work by anthropologist Earnest Hooton in the 1930s and psychologist William Sheldon in the 1940s examined physical types and their relationship to crime. Hooton looked at a whole range of attributes that criminals might be likely to have. Sheldon's work suggested that physical body type helped shape temperament and personality and that some personalities were more likely to facilitate crime. If either of these theories or Lombroso's approach worked, it would be easier to identify criminals before they committed serious crimes. Unfortunately, evidence for the validity of these physical type theories has been very weak at best.

Many social scientists, partly because of the weaknesses of early biological theories, are reluctant to specify the biological origins of criminal behavior. Advances in genetics, nutrition, and neurology may cause some to reevaluate their position. One example is the study of the relationship between an XYY chromosome pattern and violent behavior. It has been suggested that having an extra Y chromosome, an unusual occurrence, leads to violence and antisocial actions. But recent studies show that the relationship is questionable.

Despite the controversy about the XYY relationship to violence, the ways that other biological factors affect criminal and antisocial actions are being investigated. Studies of a genetic link to criminal behavior have been completed using Danish adoption records. They show a greater tendency for adoptees whose biological parents were convicted of a crime also to be involved in crime. And work is progressing on examining the relationships between nutrition, diet, and criminal behavior. It appears that advances in the biological sciences have opened the way for studies never before possible. The biological influence on criminal behavior should not be totally discounted.

Psychiatric and psychological theories of crime and delinquency have a long and varied history. Much can be traced to Freud's influence on the field. Updated psychoanalytic theories still suggest that crime is antisocial behavior reflecting an unconscious conflict. An imbalance between the well-known trio of the id, superego, and the ego can lead to problem behavior. Other important aspects of psychoanalytic thought would include the problems of fixation at a premature stage of development, such as narcissism. In a normal progression, various stages of human development are reached, worked through, and left behind. Occasionally an individual may fail to go beyond one developmental stage and become fixated. The narcissistic stage is one of self-centeredness, defensiveness, and striking out. Some psychoanalysts suggest that delinquency results from this fixation and its problems.

Another individual approach to criminal behavior is to focus on a personality disorder. Some emotional or personality problems contribute to criminal actions. Taken to the extreme, some suggest a psychopathic personality. Psychopaths habitually commit criminal acts with little or no remorse, have few social relationships, and usually do not respond to what normally are effective sanctions. Less serious personality disorders have been suggested as links to crime as well.

A basic question that legal scholars and the courts have to deal with is whether any conditions—biological, psychological, or social—can affect behavior to such a degree that the individual can no longer control his or her actions. If this is the case, the individual may not be responsible for his or her criminal actions. Recent cases have focused on the role of the usual factors such as insanity and extreme duress, as well as the conditions known as premenstrual tension (PMT) and post traumatic stress disorder (the Vietnam syndrome). In both instances, various courts have given limited recognition to these conditions as determinants of behavior.

For our purposes, it not only is important to understand the multiple causes of crime but also to consider the implications of the theories for effective crime prevention. Assume for a moment that each of the theories described above is accurate for a hypothetical criminal case. That is, the behavior is explained in full by one of the theories. Then what are the implications of the varied approaches? As an example, biological conditions would not respond well to punishment since they are beyond the control of the individual. Post traumatic stress and personality disorders suggest therapy rather than punishment. Of course, incarceration for the safety of the community still would be useful. From the standpoint of library security, little can be done to alter the behavior of individuals experiencing these problems. Yet it is possible to make the library setting one in which the undesirable behavior is less likely to occur or to be successfully carried out.

Emphasis on the Group

The second major focus is on theories that emphasize the group or society. Again, the range of possible explanations is wide and flexibility of application is important. The different social theories may each be useful at different times. Let us look briefly at structural theories, cultural theories, and group process theories.

In any society it is likely that some individuals or groups will have easier access to the benefits of that society than will others. This access can be based on a number of factors, including age, sex, educational level, occupation, family identity, race, and so on. Some of these characteristics will be viewed as legitimate bases to allow or disallow access to the rewards of a system; others would be considered illegitimate criteria. Regardless of legitimacy, any social system might provide different levels of opportunities for groups or individuals to succeed. Occasionally, some people's ability to succeed becomes blocked by the way in which the society is organized or treats the groups in the community. This is what sociologists call social structural disorganization. Those affected may still believe that they *should* have all the benefits the society has to offer even if they are not given equal opportunity to achieve them. So they may try to achieve these desired benefits through illegitimate means. That is, some may desire to achieve and have all or some of "the good things" described in the American dream, but cannot achieve them in the prescribed way. If such a group also believes that it is being discriminated against in a systematic manner, the society and its symbols may come to be viewed as acceptable targets of crime. Libraries may be one of the symbols of society that become defined as such appropriate targets.

At other times, with or without blocked opportunities, cultural factors may contribute to crime. A major theoretical view of crime formulated by criminologist Edwin Sutherland, the theory of differential association, suggests that criminal behavior is learned just like any other behavior. Typically, crime is learned in small, intimate groups. The mass media have now come to play an increasingly prominent role in learning about crime, which was not the case when Sutherland formulated his theory.

Learning about crime includes learning the techniques necessary for committing the crime and the attitudes and motives necessary to support criminal behavior. It is suggested that the more frequent the interaction with others who commit crimes or who hold favorable attitudes toward breaking the law, the more likely one is to engage in crime him- or herself (a frequent argument against jailing juvenile or first-time offenders with "hardened" criminals). Obviously, some neighborhoods provide greater opportunities for these interaction patterns than do others.

Some of the skills necessary for committing crime are simple, as in the case of vandalism, purse snatching, and some assaults. Other forms of crime are more complex. These more sophisticated illegal skills include hot wiring a car, some arson, forgery, identification and theft of valuable books and documents, and so on. If the skills are available, crime is even more likely to occur if it is supported by attitudes and beliefs making it acceptable to the perpetrator. These attitudes or rationalizations are known as techniques of neutralization.[6] Such rationalizations help the perpetrator to counteract the norms against committing crimes.

Two common techniques of neutralization include denial of responsibility and denial of injury. In the first, the offender claims no responsibility for the act—society, the environment, or peer pressure may be blamed. The denial of injury suggests that the victim really was not harmed—"Insurance will pay for it," "They won't miss it," "Drugs don't hurt anyone." Support for any attitude that justifies crime and violence makes these actions more likely to occur.

Many of the problems that affect libraries involve acts typically committed by juveniles. Acts of vandalism, theft, drug-related offenses, many assaults, and others are likely to be committed by the young. Although most of the theories we have summarized apply well to delinquency, there is another approach that helps us understand juvenile crime. People in groups are likely to do things they would not do as individuals. This is particularly noticeable in the behavior of the young. Much of the behavior of juveniles when in groups would not even be considered, or be possible, when alone. Why is this? Several processes known to occur in all kinds of groups may contribute to the undesirable behavior.

The most widely discussed process is peer pressure, or pressure to conform to the standards of the group. What sometimes is viewed by adults as nonconformity is really a choice to conform to peer group standards rather than to societal standards. In general terms, peer group pressure is so powerful because the group meets so many of the needs of youth. Even though young people have different needs, they may all be provided for by a peer group. And conformity to group standards may not be wholly voluntary. The leadership and patterns of power within the group may place strong demands on some members to conform to group behavior even if they prefer not to.

Many other group processes also can affect behavior. For example, when actions are carried out by a group, the individual members may not feel personally responsible for what happens. This diffusion of responsibility serves to remove the feeling of being accountable for one's actions. There also may be increased feelings of power because of the number of people involved. Actions that might be considered impossible for the lone offender would be perceived as attainable by the group. Similarly, a feeling of anonymity may exist among group members. Juveniles in areas where they are not known personally are more likely to violate standards and laws. Being in a large group may make one feel as if he or she will not be personally recognized or identified.

A striking feature of many youth subcultures or groups is a joy in taking risks. Risk taking becomes a way of gaining esteem or reputation. Some of these risks involve "legitimate" activities such as contact sports, fast biking, and dodging traffic when crossing the street. Illegitimate activities also can provide an avenue for risk taking. Driving patterns and petty theft often fit into this picture. In a group setting some youth will go to extremes in taking risks. The process tends to escalate until many in the group are trying to outdo each other. If the focus of this risk taking turns to delinquent or criminal behavior, the more dangerous and serious the actions are likely to become.

In summary, there are many explanations for the causes of crime and delinquency. Several have been shown to be relatively weak theories; others seem quite adequate for many episodes of criminal action. Anyone trying to apply theories to control or minimize crime would be advised to be flexible and heed the implications of whichever theory seems to work best.

NOTES

1. *New York Times,* July 11, 1981, p. 1.
2. *American Libraries* 14 (May 1983), p. 260.
3. *Time,* November 29, 1976, p. 21.
4. Paul Tappan, *Crime, Justice, and Correction* (New York: McGraw-Hill, 1960), p. 10.
5. Martin R. Haskell and Lewis Yablonsky, *Juvenile Delinquency,* 3rd ed. (Boston: Houghton Mifflin, 1982).
6. Gresham Sykes and David Matza, "Techniques of Neutralization: A Theory of Delinquency," *American Sociological Review* 22 (1957).

2 CRIME STUDIES

Crime is a major problem in American society. As discussed in Chapter 1, crime patterns vary according to many sets of conditions, including geographic, community, and personal factors. Much of the crime in the United States occurs in public places: schools, libraries, commercial settings, churches, recreational areas, mass transit facilities, and so on. What do we know about crime in public places? Many studies, frequently sponsored by federal agencies, have examined some crime problems. In this chapter, let us briefly look at some studies related to crime in public places. Following that is a thorough look at literature related to crime and disruption in libraries.

Much can be learned by examining studies of crime in public places other than libraries. Many of the problems are similar or spill over from one public place to another, and many of the prevention programs used in other settings may be applicable to the library.

COMMERCIAL CRIME

The most common serious crimes affecting commercial establishments are burglary, robbery, and larceny-theft. Burglary involves the unlawful entry of a structure to commit a crime; robbery occurs when force or the threat of force is used to take something from an individual. (A building is burglarized; a person is robbed.) Larceny-theft refers to the less serious offense of taking items that belong to someone else without the use of force, including bicycle theft, shoplifting, pocket picking, and so on.

Most robberies by far occur in public places. For example, of the nearly one-half million robberies reported in 1979, only about 10 percent happened in private residences. The typical location was on the street, but stores, gas stations, and shopping centers were common sites as well.

In contrast to robberies occurring in public places, only about one-third of burglaries were committed in settings where the general public was welcome. Specifically, over 20 percent of known burglaries occurred in nonresidential settings at night; 6 percent occurred in those settings during the day. Similarly, 22 percent of the known burglaries were directed against residences during the night, but 27 percent were in homes during the day. It appears that the temporarily vacant property is the favorite target of the burglar.

Using the same year of 1979 as an example, there were nearly four million reported robberies and burglaries.[1] This number, although large, is far less than the number of reported cases of larceny-theft, which totaled over six million reports for that year. More than 10 percent of them involved shoplifting from stores; nearly one-third involved theft of items and accessories from cars. Most of the cars obviously were located in public places. Library parking lots may be high-risk targets for this type of crime.

Another crime on the increase is arson. Evidence points to a rise in both the number of arson episodes and the cost of destruction. In 1980, the *Uniform Crime Reports* issued full data on arson as a serious or Type I crime. Over 115,000 cases were reported, with property damage close to one billion dollars. But total loss figures can sometimes be misleading. The average cost per arson offense was over $7,000, but, in reality, the true loss differed greatly according to type of target. For example, the average cost of a burned motor vehicle at the time was $2,172, and the average loss in an industrial site was nearly $73,000.

The most frequent site of arson, according to the *U.C.R.*, was a single-family residential structure, followed by other residential sites and storage locations. But public institutions were not immune. The *U.C.R.* indicates that 6,588 "community/public" settings were hit by arson in that year. Furthermore, over one-quarter of the single-family residences were abandoned at the time of arson, but 95 percent of the public sites were not abandoned. The average loss to these community buildings was $14,000, among the highest average loss of any target.

Interestingly, of the arson cases in which an arrest was made, over 40 percent of those charged were under the age of 18. When the target was a commercial site, 27 percent of those arrested were under 18. However, when the target was a community/public site, offenders under 18 accounted for over 57 percent of those arrested. This, in part, reflects the characteristics of those using these community institutions, such as schools and libraries.

IN SCHOOLS

Throughout the 1960s and 1970s, more and more American schools experienced increasing problems of violence and vandalism, a trend that has declined some in the 1980s. Crime in schools certainly was not a new problem even in the 1960s, but the frequency and severity of the episodes have become of great concern. The *Violent School-Safe School Report to Congress* summarized the problem in 1979.[2] Based on a nationwide study of schools, it reported that in a typical month, 282,000 students were attacked in school, 112,000 had something taken from them by force, 50 percent of the teachers experienced verbal abuse from students, and 125,000 teachers were threatened with physical harm. In this same typical month, there was an average of 42,000 cases of property damage, 2,000 cases of arson, and over 24,000 reports of vandalism. The cost of these episodes is staggering. Estimates run as high as $600 million for the vandalism alone. When viewing data on these and other crimes as they relate to the library, keep these figures in mind. Even though libraries are now experiencing unacceptable levels of crime and disruption, these levels are in no way comparable to the rates of school crime.

Other major findings of this survey showed that although teachers were less likely to be assaulted than were students, assaults against teachers were more likely to result in serious injury. In addition, the percentage of teachers reporting attacks was highest in large cities and lowest in rural areas. Teachers in junior high schools reportedly were at the highest risk of any teachers.

Offenses against the institution—theft, arson, property destruction, and so on—were highest in the Northeast and West. Unlike assault, urban and suburban schools had similar rates for property crimes. Junior and senior high schools also showed similar rates of property offenses. As might be expected, rural and elementary level schools had the least problems with school crime and vandalism, although they were not immune.

When questioned, most principals indicated that the majority of attacks and robberies were not reported; in fact, in only one-sixth of the episodes were police officially notified. This is a problem throughout the public sector. Many administrators choose not to call police unless the crime is considered very serious. What defines a crime as "very serious" varies as much as the reasons for choosing not to report. In many cases, nonreporting is simply due to a poor or nonexistent routine recording and reporting system. If such is the case, training employees to record the necessary information and filing the preliminary report with the administrator responsible would facilitate contact with the police when warranted. Local policies should clarify when a report is or is not necessary or expected.

Other findings of the school crime study may also be relevant. The risks of personal violence and personal theft were highest during regular school hours. On the other hand, breaking and entering episodes were highest on weekends and at other times when the schools were closed. These patterns are likely to be similar to the risk patterns in public libraries as well.

Within the school, specific areas were identified as of particular risk, and once again, the implications for the library seem relevant. Basically, any crowded area or one with little supervision is vulnerable. For example, hallways and stairs in between class sessions, along with bathrooms and cafeterias, seem to be the least safe areas in many schools. In public libraries, there also are areas where supervision or the chance of observation is minimal. Bathrooms, stacks, hallways, and storage areas may be high-risk locations in many libraries.

IN RELIGIOUS INSTITUTIONS

Almost any site can provide an opportunity for crime, and churches are no exception. In fact, churches offer some ideal conditions for the criminal. Most church buildings are not secure facilities. In fact, like libraries they usually encourage public entry. This, unfortunately for users, is changing in some locations. Many churches now lock their doors at nonservice times. Security systems have been added to the building and to various sites within the church or synagogue.

In addition to their relative vulnerability, many religious institutions house desirable and costly items, such as cash, silver and gold artifacts, artwork, and other valuables. Sacred scrolls kept in synagogues have become so difficult and costly to purchase that a black market has developed.

But theft is not the only crime that affects religious institutions. Acts of vandalism often are directed against churches, and the extent of the damage from these acts can be devastating for it often extends beyond broken windows and spray paint. All too often vandals ransack the entire interior, making it very difficult for the congregation to carry on its normal routine.

Of course, some acts of crime against religious institutions are motivated not by profit or desire to destroy but by prejudice or racism. Black-owned churches, synagogues, and some Catholic churches are singled out for more than a random share of attacks. Not long ago, New York City organized a special police unit to combat crimes related to religion. According to Leonard Buder in the *New York Times:*

> The formation of a special New York City police unit to combat crimes involving racial and religious prejudice, such as cross-burnings or desecrations of churches, synagogues or cemeteries, was announced yesterday by Police Commissioner Robert J. McGuire. Expressing concern about the increase in and the

seriousness of such incidents in the city and elsewhere, the Commissioner declared: "We will not tolerate this kind of activity in New York City." . . . He said that police had recorded 107 incidents of crime involving racial, religious, and ethnic prejudice so far this year . . . . Last month, vandals broke into the Young Israel Synagogue in Willowbrook, S.I. [Staten Island], and painted swastikas and the word "Jew" on the walls. Other vandals entered the Chab Zedek Congregation in Brooklyn and stole prayer shawls and silver ornaments from Torahs. In April, 300 gravestones were toppled at St. Michael's Cemetery in Elmhurst, Queens. The year before vandals knocked over 800 headstones in Mt. Hebron Cemetery in Flushing, Queens, and 650 headstones at two Jewish cemeteries on Staten Island.[3]

This was not an isolated set of incidents. Several months later, Catholic churches and convents in the city tightened their security procedures following violent crimes against a priest and a nun.

Episodes in the Boston area illustrate the impact of crime against churches. Not long ago, vandals caused thousands of dollars worth of damage by breaking windows, damaging the altar, and stealing statues from a Dorchester church. The symbolic nature of an attack on a religious institution often extends the impact beyond the actual losses, as noted in the statements of church members. "It's God's house. Why would anyone want to steal anything from that?" "There's no reason for it." "I'll do anything to help—clean up, carpentry, anything."[4] The reactions of area residents and parishioners to an attack on their church are different from reactions to an attack on the local supermarket or bus station. Different settings mean different things to those who use them.

These problems are not limited to our largest cities. Nor are they limited to acts of theft and property destruction. Religious personnel themselves have become a target of crime. Attacks against clergy appear to be increasing. In some cases robbery seems to be the motive; in other cases sexual assaults have taken place within the institution grounds. Murders of missionaries and other religious personnel in South America and around the world, as well as in the United States, have drawn attention to the risks surrounding religious work.

PUBLIC TRANSPORTATION

The United States has a highly developed mass transit system. Unfortunately, portions of it are not as efficient as they might be and are plagued by problems of increasing deterioration and decreasing safety. Other parts of the system, including some interstate highways and air service, are relatively new and not yet suffering from serious decay. Yet even these relatively recent additions must contend with crime and disruption. For example, in 1980 United States civil aviation facilities received nearly 1,500 bomb threats and experienced 22 hijackings. Other crimes occur frequently as well. Nearly 40,000 thefts from railroads in the United States and Canada were reported in 1980, as well as more than 40,000 acts of vandalism against these same carriers. And this does not take into account crimes against passengers using rail and air facilities.

One of the most striking features of crime against public transportation facilities and their users is the random nature of the acts. Victims tend to be singled out merely by being in a particular location at a particular time. The crimes are often acts of convenience—committed because the setting provides the opportunity. Most major cities suffer some level of crime against mass transit facilities. Recent increases in transit crime in Boston, for example, brought the following reactions:

> MBTA Police Chief Richard Whelan, after three beatings of MBTA bus drivers in Roxbury and Dorchester last Saturday night, said Authority plans to equip busses with radios is an important step in curbing violence on those vehicles. Saturday's attacks occurred as follows. . . . was beaten and struck with beer bottles. . . . The reason: The men were angry because the rear door of the bus would not open. . . . was struck in the face by a beer bottle by one of four men. . . . The reason: Gillis told them to pay their fare before leaving the bus. . . . assaulted by a gang of 15 teenagers on his bus. . . . dragged from the bus, hit with a blunt instrument, pushed and kicked and robbed of his wrist watch and glasses. . . . The reason: None apparent.[5]

Reactions to the attacks were to increase the transit police force by ten officers, initiate a program to increase public awareness of the problem, and install a new flashing light warning system. So in addition to the cost of the crimes themselves, there are additional costs related to prevention and fear of crime.

RECREATIONAL AREAS

There is an interesting contrast in the problem of crime in recreational areas. On one hand, these are the places where people go to relax and get away from daily problems. On the other hand, recreational areas have certain characteristics that facilitate crime.

What are public recreational areas? Among the variety of settings that could be considered are beaches, parks, campgrounds, municipal golf courses and pools, sports stadiums, and national parks and monuments. What do these areas have in common that might foster crime? For one thing, many visitors at these locations tend to be thinking about anything except becoming a crime victim. Generally, people on vacation or day trips are not as careful about crime prevention as they are at home or work. Second, these locations often are crowded, giving the potential offender many suitable targets. Furthermore, there are many distractions to cover up crime episodes. When people use recreational areas, they often bring valuable goods with them, but they don't always keep close watch on their possessions. Behavior patterns at beaches illustrate this point. The territory that people stake out tends to be littered with radios, tape recorders, clothing, jewelry, and other valuable items. What better place for the thief to operate? Finally, security at many recreational areas is minimal. This is particularly crucial when the area also is an isolated site, such as a national park. Crimes in national parks tend to be mostly cases of theft or burglary, although crimes of violence do occur. In 1979 there were 15 homicides and nearly 100 rapes in national parks reported to federal authorities. There were also over 6,000 cases of larceny-theft. Drug-related problems are another concern among officials responsible for the security of the park system. Incidents in the nation's capital have been particularly troublesome, due in part to an understaffed security force.

Some recreational areas obviously attract people looking for more than relaxation. The Spring College Weekend at Florida beaches is an example. These festivities usually result in hundreds of arrests, many for disorderly conduct. But crimes of violence do occur and theft is common.

Crimes of violence are most likely to occur when participants expect to be able to do whatever they want to do—their expectations for freedom are high, as the case with the college students. According to Hillery and Lincoln, if such expectations are met with restrictions on behavior, assaults are more likely to occur. This is true not only at Ft. Lauderdale, but at Mardi Gras time as well.[6] Apparently, some people react aggressively to what they see as unnecessary controls. It is possible that students or library patrons who feel that their behavior is unfairly restricted will strike out against the institution or its personnel. This may help to explain some cases of vandalism, particularly by young patrons.

IN LIBRARIES

Early Concerns

It is difficult to determine when the professional community began to be aware of library crime as a problem. Certainly book theft had occurred in many libraries for many years: But defining these thefts and other criminal activities in the library as "a problem to be dealt with" is a fairly recent phenomenon. Giving voice to a problem long after it is known is not uncommon, however. For example, the problems of child abuse and spouse abuse only recently have been defined by many as a social problem despite the fact that these behaviors were prevalent well before the 1960s and 1970s.

One way to measure when something is recognized as a problem is to examine the professional literature. A good starting point for library crime is the relatively early article by Ralph Munn in *Library Journal*, 1935. According to Munn, although book theft was already an old problem by that year, it was not widely discussed by librarians. To some extent this is still true. At least many librarians still prefer not to talk about it.

Some administrators apparently simply accept some level of book theft as unavoidable and a problem that tends to "go with the territory." This implies that prevention is not feasible given the resources of the institution. (As indicated in Chapter 6, even with limited resources the level of theft may be reduced, sometimes dramatically.) This feeling of helplessness was expressed by Munn:

> In considering theft, I believe that we must admit at the outset that we are quite helpless against the real thief who is determined to steal, since it is not desirable to lock up our books nor possible to search every one who leaves the building. Fortunately, the average library does not attract the professional thief, and those libraries which have real treasures can take special means of protecting them. All of us, however, suffer from the pilfering of more casual thieves—students, gangs of boys, and individuals who are occasionally tempted to steal.[7]

Early suggestions for controlling book theft are still relevant despite their simplicity. Exit controls, architectural planning, prosecution when necessary, and education were mentioned by Munn as potential deterrents. When coupled with advances in technology and newer theories of crime prevention, these are indeed still useful suggestions.

Before Munn's article, very little attention was paid to the problems of theft and mutilation of books. Earlier work suggested that there might have been a problem, but the fact that actual thefts were involved was not clearly stated. For example, a 1917 issue of *Library Journal* contains an article dealing with a simplified form of inventory:

> The taking of inventory has become so onerous in large libraries that some are omitting it altogether, or taking it only at long intervals. This course seems indefensible in the case of the custodianship of public property. . . . The number of volumes in the library was found to be 488,224 which would indicate a loss of 1113 volumes during the year—rather small for so large a library.[8]

It is not clear whether the lost volumes were stolen, overdue, or actually lost. What is important is the recommendation to maintain accurate and timely records of missing inventory.

Ten years later, *Library Journal* once again dealt with the inventory problem. Replies to an American Library Association (ALA) survey on inventory practices indicated that there was movement away from complete annual inventories. Biennial inventories and inventories of "special sections" were reported to be more popular. Furthermore, some libraries reportedly had done away with inventories altogether.

> The University of Pennsylvania considers that the cost is not justified by results. When a book is missing, the fact is reported to a member of the shelf and stack department, whose chief business is searching. If the missing volume is not found and it is urgently needed, another copy is bought or borrowed. If the need is not urgent, the title goes on the "missing list" and remains there (being searched for now and then) for fifteen months. If it is not found then, it is considered lost, and the cards are removed from the catalog unless decision is made to replace the book.[9]

Vandalism and Mutilation

The first major problem that research for this book investigated was the range and frequency of various acts of vandalism. There appears to be no limit to the form that vandalism can take. The imagination of the individual vandal is unfortunately quite vivid.

Most public buildings experience some acts of vandalism on occasion. These destructive acts not only cause some immediate damage, but they tend to have longer range effects on those witnessing the vandalism. This may be particularly true in a public or other library. If the general public expects libraries to be safe and crime-free, these visible acts serve to remind them that their perceptions are wrong. Not only are their perceptions wrong, but it may appear to them as if no target is safe. After all, "If the library is being victimized, what is the society coming to?" In other words, the same act may have different consequences depending on where it occurs. Crime against the library, when visible to the public, may extend far beyond its immediate impact in terms of shaping people's attitudes about their community.

What do we know about vandalism in general and vandalism against libraries in particular? According to Colin Ward:

> The human environment is subject to every kind of wear, decay, attrition, erosion, change, renewal and destruction, some of which we label vandalism. Those who earn a living by modifying the environment have an interest in the durability of their handiwork, those charged with its maintenance are usually

> concerned with its survival, those who inhabit it are expected to show some degree of care for it. Consequently we all have opinions on vandalism. We all know the vandal. He is somebody else. In general terms he is someone whose activities in the environment we deplore. . . . The stereotype of the vandal . . . is that of a working class male adolescent, and his act is the "wanton," "senseless," or "motiveless" destruction of property, usually public property of some kind. He and his behavior constitute a "social problem."[10]

There is a great deal of truth to Ward's comments. Yet the stereotype may be just that, a stereotype, with some accurate components and some obvious inaccuracies. Vandals do tend to be young, but it is not clear that they still tend to be solely male. Furthermore, many acts of vandalism occur in small groups. Youth tend to reinforce each other's acts of destruction.

What kinds of destruction are libraries and other public buildings likely to suffer? Certainly the most common involve the things we see every day as we walk through almost any neighborhood—broken windows, graffiti, and minor acts of damage to buildings, cars, fences, and so on. But the problem does not stop there. In addition, libraries are likely to suffer other kinds of destruction due to the nature of their operations and facilities. The intentional mutilation of books and other resource material is one such problem.

One of the most troublesome and costly problems faced by many libraries is mutilation of materials. Let us look at three important issues related to this problem: characteristics of the offender, situational factors conducive to these actions, and preferred target. Some prevention measures are examined here; others are discussed in Chapter 6.

Is there any evidence that people who mutilate books and other materials in libraries are different from those who do not? That is, do they differ in a psychological or social way from nonoffenders? According to Weiss, there are psychological and sociological factors that influence the choice to steal or mutilate books and periodicals: "An attempt was made to identify the personal characteristics of university students who mutilated and/or did not check out library books different from student-body members who followed normal library-use behavior."[11]

Earlier studies by Hendrick and Murfin found that situational factors played an important role in influencing the choice to mutilate. Personal differences between mutilators and nonmutilators were minimal. Rather, those who mutilated periodicals claimed to be influenced by such things as not having enough time because the library was closing, not having or not wanting to spend the money to make copies of the needed material, or the copy machine was not working properly.[12] Weiss's study was similar, but as suggested: ". . . this study occurred in a different sociocultural time frame. The Hendrick and Murfin study was done in 1973 and this one in

1978. This is an important difference for library book abuse because the two times compare student activity in the library before and after the copy machine 'revolution.' "[13]

Weiss's findings are based on a convenience sample of undergraduate students. Less than 10 percent of the sample admitted to failure to properly check out books at least once; about the same proportion (9 percent) said that they had torn pages out of books or periodicals. These proportions are similar to those reported by Hendrick and Murfin. They found that 8 percent of the sample admitted mutilating journals.

How do the rule breakers differ from the rule followers? One major difference was in reported academic performance. Those who admitted stealing and/or mutilating were more likely to report that they were doing very well academically. This could be both a motive to steal and in part a cause of the good performance. A failure to consider the needs of others also was characteristic of this group. Financial need, the perceived quality of service by the library, and avoiding copying costs did not appear to be major reasons for theft and mutilation. On the other hand, the offenders generally believed that the chances of being caught were slight, and those who stole books were slightly more likely to steal other things. Weiss found:

> . . . the norm-violating behavior to be caused not primarily by the more external library service but by a psychological and sociological state within the students who commit such acts . . . believe that there is a definite antisocial streak that is destructive. . . . Students who break the library rules in this way do so because of their coping response to do well under academic pressures.[14]

Souter found that delinquent patrons tended to have or to create problems outside the library.

> Firstly, their selfish attitude makes itself felt in the university as a whole. Thus at two of the libraries visited the following point was made: "The curious thing is that many of these [delinquent readers] are also in trouble in other parts of the university. . . . You ring up and say: 'Can you tell me anything about [—]?' [and] the name is known wherever you ring, whether it's the domestic bursar, the secretary for student . . . affairs, and they may be very charming people, but they're just a pain in the neck to everyone." Secondly, it appears that delinquent readers take their disagreeable tendencies outside the university altogether. . . . There are very strong indications that there are some selfish individuals in today's universities who take what they want in any way they can, and feel justified in so doing. They do this indiscriminately, in a library context, in a university context, and in the context of society as a whole. . . . Their intention is simply to benefit themselves. But they do not care about others. . . .[15]

Academic pressures or concern about achievement are problems that affect all ages. Pressure placed on employees to achieve and produce, often within a limited time frame, are not unlike those placed on college students. The academic demands placed on those below college age can also lead to anxiety about school assignments. Some assignments might lead to more temptation to mutilate library materials than will others. This is not a new problem. In his early paper on book theft and mutilation, Munn writes about the problem of mutilation facilitated by assigning students the task of illustrating their reports with magazine photographs.

> To most of us these days, however, mutilation means just one thing—the illustrated notebook made by students as a school requirement under the project method of teaching. During the last few years this school requirement has advanced mutilation from a serious but relatively minor difficulty, to one which threatens the very existence of our book collections. . . . Warnings to students had little effect, and teachers were unable or too busy to verify the origins of pictures. In Newark the Library then secured a school order which prohibited teachers from accepting pictures cut from books. . . . Brookline, Massachusetts, went further in outlawing both book and magazine material. . . . Pittsburgh and Baltimore went the whole distance in securing orders which prohibit the use of illustrated notebooks entirely.[16]

Apparently the problem still exists. Despite the availability of photocopying equipment, both the cost involved and the relative unattractiveness of black and white compared to full color originals encourage juveniles to mutilate periodicals. According to a notation in *Library and Archival Security:*

> Mutilation in the young adult section plagues most public libraries, as well as school libraries, so some of our readers may wish to consider an informal idea used by the East Islip Public Library. A "give-away" file is maintained for youngsters, and consists of pictures clipped from different magazines which were donated or else about to be thrown away. Pictures are also taken from old or incomplete sets of encyclopedias.[17]

Reports from East Islip indicated that the program seems to help cut down on mutilation of journals. This is a good example of simple and low-cost action that does have an impact. However, there may be one hidden danger in this type of program. Are the young students getting mixed messages? Although they are being told that it is inappropriate for them to mutilate periodicals, they are being given the remnants of periodicals mutilated by others! This may give the impression that it is all right for adults to do this, but not for children. The use of incomplete encyclopedias may be even more confusing. Will young children be able to discriminate between discarded volumes and current holdings the next time they need a specific picture and cannot find it in the giveaways?

Considerable evidence suggests that some types of crimes are influenced by a "modeling effect." That is, witnessing the crime or evidence of the crime may induce others to commit the same crime or similar crimes. Examples include the rapid increase in airline hijackings in the 1960s. Between 1930 and 1967, there were just 9 hijackings of American aircraft. But in 1969 there were 40. The tide was slowed with the passage of legislation increasing security and facilitating prosecution of offenders. By 1973 there was 1 attempt. However, in the early 1980s a relaxing of security may have been responsible for another rash of hijackings. Similarly, the "Tylenol killings" spawned a rash of "copycat" offenses. A variety of products from nose spray to candy have been tampered with. And chances are that most if not all of them were the direct result of modeling of the initial, highly publicized Tylenol case. This points out the major dilemma with the modeling effect. At what point does the need to inform the public for their own safety become a danger in its own right?

Arsonists and vandals also may be affected by modeling. And the presence of graffiti surely encourages more graffiti. A major argument regarding crime and violence on television is that exposure may increase the likelihood of the viewer subsequently committing violent acts.

Are rates of periodical and book mutilation affected by exposure to evidence of past acts of vandalism? Apparently so. According to Gouke and Murfin:

> We attempted to determine whether the presence of mutilated or damaged volumes on the shelves affected the rate of mutilation. Since volumes at the centralized library were checked once in 1973 and once again in 1977, it was possible to see whether those volumes which were "clean" or undamaged at first examination, or those which were obviously mutilated, most often received further damage in the ensuing three and a half years. It was found that 87 percent of obviously mutilated volumes received further damage, while only 67 percent of "clean" volumes did so. It appeared that leaving ripped out and unrepaired volumes on the shelves did lead to an increased rate of mutilation.[18]

It is interesting that the authors perceived that "only" 67 percent of clean volumes were mutilated. This is in itself an unacceptably high rate.

There is further evidence that mutilation is affected by modeling. Interviews with known mutilators have shown that exposure to earlier acts motivated them to do the same. "To some extent, then, a hostile-aggressive motivation may be a determining factor." Some claimed that one way of getting even with other student mutilators and the library was to mutilate again. The respondents indicated that a volume with missing articles was already ruined, but that they would be less likely to cut from an untouched volume or from a book.[19]

Mutilation of library materials occurs in every type of library. The effects of damaged and missing material are widespread but perhaps nowhere as strong as in academic libraries. Hendrick and Murfin claim that approximately three-quarters of students at two different universities were inconvenienced by mutilated materials. Recall the suggestion by Weiss that admitted offenders tended to be doing very well academically. The combination of pressure to maintain quality academic work and the inconvenience of mutilated material could lead to increased pressures to further destroy needed materials. Murfin and Hendrick illustrate this frustration in their research: "Better get it before it's gone" and "Everybody else is ripping out."[20]

In these examples, students are quoted, but there is no reason to exclude faculty, who also are under pressure for quality performance, from the list of potential offenders. One possible pattern to consider is that even though a small proportion of patrons is involved, some are repeat offenders. That is, a few may be responsible for a sizable amount of damage. Research on other types of crime and delinquency supports this view. A small group of repeat offenders may be responsible for a majority of the vandalism, burglaries, or car thefts in a community. Do mutilators tend to be repeaters as well? Several surveys and case studies indicate yes. Hoppe and Simmel describe one such case.

> In the Spring of 1967 a pair of students who were in Miami University's new undergraduate library noticed a fellow student systematically tearing pages from a volume and placing them in his own notebook. The couple followed the culprit, reported him, and assisted in his apprehension. Investigation revealed that this was not the first time he had behaved this way. Apparently he had a habit of obtaining his material for study by removing the needed pages from the books they were in and thereby avoiding the bother of checking the books out and worrying about them becoming overdue.[21]

This type of mutilation serves another function for the offender. In addition to being more convenient from his or her perspective, the removal of materials prevents other students from having equal access to vital material. For those students who are academically selfish, this may be perceived as a way of improving one's own relative performance within the classroom. The mutilator's grades may be seen as staying up, with the advantage of others' grades being threatened.

Occasionally these offenders take on the characteristics of "collectors." In these cases the offender may strike at more than one institution to increase the size of his or her own collection. The case of "Jock the Ripper" (see Figure 2) involved not only several institutions but libraries in several states as well.

Since mutilation is so widespread and subject to the special interests of the mutilator, are there any regularities in target selection? Certainly expen-

"Jock the Ripper" Is Apprehended in South Dakota

A one month clipping spree pulled off by "Jock the Ripper," a man who ravaged college yearbooks and newspapers in three states for football player and action photos, ended abruptly when South Dakota State police—tipped off by a Black Hills State College librarian—found him studiously cutting out yearbook photos. The crew-cut, heavy-set young man was taken to the Deadwood, South Dakota jail and booked on charges of malicious mischief. At the time of his arrest, he had in his possession $2600 in bills and a pistol as well as scores of photos—which he offered to return to the library.

Robert Perrin, director of North Dakota's Jamestown College Library, alerted area libraries by teletype when he discovered damage to the library collection amounting to some $600. The interlibrary loan teletype became clogged with messages by mid-morning as schools in the state surveyed back issues of annuals and newspapers and replied. Damages were reported by the University of North Dakota, North Dakota State University, Valley City State, Dickinson State, Minot State, Mayville State, Bismarck Junior College, and the Wahpeton State School of Science.

In Minnesota, similar reports later came from Concordia College, Morehead State, Morris State, and Bemidji State College. In South Dakota reports of vandalism came from Yankton College, Northern State University, and the University of South Dakota at Springfield and at Huron.

Colleges were not the only institution hit by "Jock the Ripper." The *Jamestown Sun* discovered at least five instances where clippings had been apparently razored out of its bound volumes, covering sports events of the last two years. A report from Yankton, South Dakota indicated that "Jock" may have been a visitor at *The Press and Dakotan* there. The alleged vandal's notebook—containing diary-like entries resembling an itinerary—were found in the newspaper offices.

North Dakota college librarians estimate that their damages will amount to well over $10,000, and one librarian pointed out that a great many of the yearbooks damaged are irreplaceable.

A spokesman for the University of North Dakota has announced that that institution intends to prosecute the alleged vandal. Attorney Charles Gilje, however, pointed out that the charge now filed against the vandal is a misdemeanor and that agencies in North Dakota cannot ask for extradition unless a felony is at issue. He suggested that North Dakota libraries consolidate charges in the matter to facilitate the extradition. At last report, all North Dakota colleges affected have agreed to file charges through the University of North Dakota.

■ Figure 2 From *Library Journal,* September 1, 1972.

sive reference materials often are singled out. Back in 1960, Emerson pointed out:

> ITEM: The 8th edition of the *Directory of Medical Specialists* had pages covering the local internal medical specialists torn out within a week after it had been placed on the shelf. . . . ITEM: Almost all books containing photos of German aircraft of World War II have had these sections ripped out. . . .
> ITEM: Fairborn's *Book of Crests* has so many crests cut out it looks as if someone were trying to devise an information retrieval system based on a punched book![22]

Similar conclusions were made by Zimmerman in 1961. He claimed that no library book was immune from mutilation, but that some categories were more likely to be targets than were others. "They include encyclopedias, photographic books, more specifically art books containing plates, medical and/or sex books. . . ."[23] A 1973 study at Temple University in Philadelphia found that 21 of a select group of 107 journals were extensively damaged, and over half had lost a few articles each. The most frequently damaged journals were in education and psychology.[24]

Research conducted on patterns of mutilation of books in English university libraries found that "All physical forms are vulnerable. . . . So are all subject fields but some more often attacked than others."[25] In particular, social science materials appeared to be among the hardest hit. Popular periodicals also appear to have been favorite targets. Gouke and Murfin reported that "For example, in one 1965 volume of *Reader's Digest* checked in 1973, 83 percent of the issues were mutilated, and in a similar volume of *Psychology Today,* 65 percent of the issues were mutilated. Certain older issues of *Time* and *Sports Illustrated* had even achieved the dubious distinction of having 100 percent of the issues mutilated."[26] And note the problem of one Ohio university (see Figure 3).

Souter continues with a description of general causes of reader delinquency, including the library, the offender, and other library patrons. Important library-related factors include security, availability of an item, quality of photocopying services, and the type of sanctions that could be imposed. Several of these are similar to the situational factors discussed by Weiss and Hendrick and Murfin. In the Weiss study, situational factors were not as important as personal factors, but the Hendrick and Murfin study does give some support to the importance of situational factors as determinants of crime patterns. Several of the students interviewed about mutilating books said that the episode occurred "just before the library closed." All those interviewed noted that they did the damage in study carrels, suggesting that selected placement and systematic surveillance of carrels might deter some mutilation. These factors, along with earlier damage serving as a model, support the potential importance of situational factors.

Massive Mutilation at Case

In the newsletter of Case Western Reserve University Libraries, Sears Library Periodicals Librarian Michale Murphy reports "the single largest mutilation in years": over 1000 pages were razored out of two bound volumes of medical journals as well as a number of current journals. The mutilated volumes are *Biomaterials, Medical Devices, and Artificial Organs* and the *Journal of Biomedical Materials Research*. The cost of replacing the volumes could run as high as several thousand dollars, remarks Murphy, because the items are now out of print and there is no market price.

■ Figure 3 From *Library Journal*, September 15, 1982, p. 1678.

Notice, however, that situational factors are simply that—situational. The critical conditions vary from library to library, and what may facilitate crime under one set of conditions may not do so when coupled with a different set of conditions. For example, if mutilation peaks just before closing in one library, perhaps in that setting the temporary high demand for photocopying or for change exceeds the available resources. In another facility these resources may be adequate and there is no substantial increase in last-minute damage to materials.

What is the role of other library patrons in encouraging or discouraging mutilation of materials? One major issue is the willingness of nonmutilators to take an active role in trying to prevent or reduce the destruction. In a more general sense, the unwillingness of bystanders to help prevent crime is a serious problem. There are many reasons why people who observe crimes are reluctant to become involved. These range from a belief that the criminal justice system will do nothing to the offender to fear for one's own personal safety. In addition, many bystanders indicate "They don't have time," "It was none of their business," "They weren't sure that something was wrong," and "They thought someone else would take care of it." Encouraging observers of crime to become actively involved is difficult. Many people in our society have been taught to "mind their own business" and to "respect other people's privacy and property." Intervening in a potential crime situation requires overcoming these prohibitions as well as concern for personal safety. Furthermore, the situation in question must first be defined as one needing our assistance. We must perceive and believe that something is wrong before we can consider what action, if any, to take.

Hoppe and Simmel examined the reactions of passive bystanders to book-ripping. In their study, they staged episodes of intentional book damage in both the old and the new libraries of Miami University. Since the new library was designed in part to make students feel more responsible for the facility and its contents, it was predicted that this library environment would affect reactions to damage. Easy access to materials and a relaxed atmosphere were major features of the new facility. The book-ripping episode was staged by having a male accomplice approach the stacks near the subjects. The accomplice selected the book used as a prop and after looking at it for one minute proceeded to rip out a page. Over a period of three minutes, six pages were ripped out. The accomplice then left the area. An observer stationed nearby interviewed and explained the experiment to any subject who made contact with the offender or sought out a librarian. Subjects who made no overt responses were interviewed ten minutes after the episode. Only 9 of 82 subjects made any overt response. Of these, 7 tried to find a librarian and only one made contact with the accomplice. Unexpectedly, students in the old library were more likely to respond than were students in the new library. The authors claim that this may have been due to a greater awareness of the episode. Hoppe and Simmel express their concern over the small proportion of interveners because:

> It should be remembered that the stooge was not trying to hide his act but was ripping several pages from what was apparently a library book while studying very close to a student or group of students. It is particularly disquieting to ponder the likely proportion of responses which would occur when one was truly pilfering pages from a library book.[27]

Students who noticed the infraction but chose not to get involved gave the familiar reasons, including noninvolvement ("I didn't care," "It was none of my business") and the perception that nothing was wrong because the stooge must have had permission or that it was not a library book.

Anything that would increase the likelihood of observers reporting destructive acts would be helpful. Based on other studies of crime reporting, several factors should be considered. One, the rules should be clear regarding mutilation. There should be no ambiguity in the minds of patrons about the inappropriateness of such actions. Two, a safe procedure for intervention must be devised. Notifying a library employee is one of the least threatening responses a patron can make. Allowing for an anonymous report will reduce concern about becoming "too involved." Furthermore, it is important to indicate to patrons the difficulty in replacing damaged materials, thereby increasing the possibility that the observer will feel inconvenienced by mutilators. Finally, publicize the successful apprehensions of mutilators. This will encourage reporting by showing patrons that their actions can be effective. Publicity may also deter potential offenders. Just posting the rules and regulations, although usually helpful, does not

WILLFUL MUTILATION OF ~~LIBRARY~~ *melissa's* MATERIAL IS A SERIOUS CRIME !!!

**NEW HAMPSHIRE
REVISED STATUTES ANNOTATED**

572:42-a (NEW) OFFENSES AGAINST ~~LIBRARIES~~ *melissa*
Any person who shall willfully or maliciously deface, damage or destroy any property belonging to or in the care of any gallery or museum or any state, public, school, college, or other institutional library, shall be fined not more than three hundred dollars. Any such person shall forfeit to or for the use of such library, gallery, or museum, three times the amount of the damage sustained, to be recovered in an action of the superior court.
Source: 1959, 60: 1, eff. June 20, 1959.

■ Figure 4

always result in decreased mutilation. Potential offenders must view the situation seriously, unfortunately not the case shown in Figure 4.

It seems that at least three sets of personal factors influence a patron's decision to mutilate library materials. These factors function in addition to the situational conditions and the responses of other patrons. They include the need for and interest in the item and its perceived market value. Need for the item is influenced by the pressures of work assignments, student assignments, and professional concerns such as research and writing. Although the item is needed by the patron, it is not inherently more valuable than any other item. Much of the mutilation caused by students falls into this category. Once again, by either decreasing the need for the item

> ## Security & the Rising Cost of Rare Documents
> One medical librarian told *LJ* that it is extremely likely that large universities—which have suffered gigantic book losses through theft —as well as medical libraries will become more and more the objects of sneak attack simply because the cost of rare documents has risen sharply in the past few years. Medical pamphlets published in the 1900's once went for a few dollars, he pointed out, and now each is selling for around $200. The rising costs of rare documents, he said, could very well bring about a new rash of major book thefts.
>
> ■ Figure 5 From *Library Journal*, September 15, 1973, p. 1866.

(altering assignments) or providing reasonable alternatives (reserves, photocopying, multiple copies, and the like), the pressures to mutilate materials may be reduced. Converting high-risk items to microfilm or microform is one reasonable alternative that should reduce the risk of mutilation or theft. Meiboom noted that after converting the periodicals of a hospital library to microform, the amount of damage to them declined.[28]

Perhaps more difficult to deal with because of its unpredictability is the damage carried out by those who are "collecting" material on specific topics. The range of potential topics is limited only by the interests of the offenders. Some care can be taken to give special protection to materials dealing with inherently high interest areas. These might include genealogies, works and photographs of any heroic or cult figures, such as music and movie celebrities, dictators, and locally idolized athletes. Materials that relate to hobbies and collectibles are themselves prone to misuse.

The collector, although highly motivated, may be easier to deter than those who damage materials for financial gain. Items that have market value even when not intact are particularly vulnerable, such as some works of art and rare books, manuscripts, and documents (see Figure 5). In addition, some less obvious materials may be singled out. Winslow Homer illustrations were removed from books and journals in several libraries. One major public library reported loss of the entire collection of Norman Rockwell covers from the *Saturday Evening Post*.

Deterring those who mutilate for profit is perhaps the most difficult, but there is one possibility to consider. The "professional" thief is perhaps the most rational of those who mutilate, at least in terms of calculating risks and payoffs. Any program that increases the chance of apprehension and punishment is likely to have some impact on this type of offender. Even though it may be difficult to protect all materials at risk, increasing surveillance or making observation more likely can be effective.

Book Theft

One recurring claim made in library literature is that the theft of manuscripts or books is almost as old as libraries themselves. Perhaps it is the magnitude of the problem that has changed in recent years. According to Munn:

> When the Persians went into Egypt and withdrew papyri from the library of Rameses II, without stopping for any formalities at the charging desk, they began a practice which has remained to torment libraries ever since. Book theft is thus as old as libraries themselves. It might almost be listed as one of the original and basic sins of mankind. . . .[29]

Similarly, in an article examining the ethical and economic issues involved in library theft, Culp suggests that "Those who have had a nodding acquaintance with the history of libraries will recall that books were at one time chained to library tables. These volumes had been painstakingly produced one at a time, and the need for the conservation was manifest."[30] And Paris notes that "Priceless library holdings were once protected by heavy chains. Wales' Hereford Cathedral stands as a silent reminder of this effective theft-preventive measure of the past—more than 1,400 volumes and manuscripts are attached by chains to rods on the 17th century book presses."[31]

Interestingly, we still chain resources to library tables. However, now those resources tend to be audiovisual equipment, microcomputers, and OCLC terminals. In some ways the more things change, the more they stay the same.

How prevalent is book theft? Has the rate increased in recent years? How much does book theft cost the nation's libraries? These are crucial but difficult questions to answer. Most existing studies focus on a single institution. Furthermore, the typical study looks at a limited time period. To describe trends in book theft requires a long-term study with a representative cross section of libraries. Data in Chapter 3 provide information from the cross section, but are limited in the time frame. Only two states were sampled a second time to allow for an analysis of crime trends across time. Longitudinal studies are costly and time-consuming. Yet given the probable losses in books and other materials, such studies could be cost-effective in the long run.

What is already known about the incidence of book theft? Is there a typical loss rate or does it vary from library to library or by type of library? Studies suggest variation may be the norm, not only from one library to another but within a single library from one time to another. Variation between different parts of the collection also occurs with some regularity. In a study conducted at the University of California, a sampling of books in the collection was examined because:

The staff felt that significant losses were occurring in the collection. They based their feelings upon their work with patrons in trying to locate wanted items which were listed as part of the collection but could not be accounted for when searched. . . . A full-fledged inventory of the collection was not possible because: a) financial resources for this would not be available, and b) the collection was highly used.[32]

Based on the survey findings, Kaske reports that although only 2 percent of the books in the sample had been reported missing, over 13 percent actually were missing as a result of assumed theft. Notice that this does not mean that 13 percent were stolen that year, but rather that 13 percent were stolen over some unspecified time period. The actual rate of loss was not determined in this study. It was shown, however, that certain categories of books were more likely to disappear than others. One popular topic exhibited a 78 percent loss of books in the collection.

Souter's study of theft and other problems in British universities also indicates that the magnitude of the problem varies from one location to another. The average annual rate of loss in British academic libraries was estimated to be 1.5 percent of the total collection. Estimates of losses from open shelves were almost twice as high. Once again there was marked institutional variation. For one year, Edinburgh University reported a loss of less than one-tenth of 1 percent, which was just slightly lower than the rate in Glasgow University. At the other extreme, losses at Liverpool Polytechnic Humanities Library were 5 percent per year. Also according to Souter:

At University College Swansea Library in 1970 it was found that 773 items were newly missing—against 563 in 1969. At Strathclyde University Library the figure for 1970–71 was 822 as against 696 for 1969–70; while Stirling University Library's figure for 1970–71 was 985—more than double the 405 of the previous year.[33]

The *Carnegie Report on Fair Practices in Higher Education* suggested that book losses of U.S. universities may be higher than those in Great Britain.

. . . the undergraduate libraries at the University of California–Berkeley, Northwestern, and the University of Washington reported annual loss rates of from two to five percent. Tufts University found that almost eight percent of the books in its libraries disappear after just one year on the shelves . . . and an inventory at the University of Maryland found losses of more than 30,000 volumes. For a three year period, UC Berkeley reported losses of 12 percent of its 150,000 volume undergraduate collection. . . . And one study said that it would cost no less than $63.7 million (plus processing costs) each year if only one percent of library collections were stolen.[34]

> ### Big Losses for Tucson
> Arizona's Tucson Public Library reports that a CLSI Bar Coding project conducted by Comprehensive Employment and Training Act staffers has pinpointed book losses at its Woods branch at 17 percent (16,535 volumes). TPL notes that this loss figure matches that found when its Wilmot branch was inventoried, and it could well be the average for all TPL branches. And loss figures for nonprint materials were even worse: 54 percent (3,590) of the Woods collection was missing, with highest losses (64 percent) in the records collection. At Wilmot, nonprint losses were pegged at 52 percent.
>
> ■ Figure 6 From *Library Journal,* April 15, 1979, p. 878.

Any estimates of theft rates should be made with care. According to a study by Niland and Kurth, many volumes identified as stolen may not be. Repeated searches for 5,459 lost volumes over a three-year period in the Washington University library reduced the apparent loss rate by 40 percent. The annual loss rate was estimated after taking into account intended deletions in the shelf list and the growth rate of the collection. The new revised annual loss rate was then estimated at .35 percent, far lower than the original estimate of lost volumes. There was, however, variation in this figure when examining the losses of the art and architecture library; there the rate was over 2.5 percent. Niland and Kurth suggest that this was due to both the attractiveness of the volumes and the lack of proper exit controls in the art and architecture library.[35] Other libraries suffer big losses too, as, for example, in Figure 6.

How does the rate of book theft in college and university libraries compare with the rate in other facilities, such as public schools and public libraries? Vinnes's study of two urban high schools, conducted in the 1960s, has interest today. He found that the proportion of books lost was comparable to the rates reported in studies of college and university libraries. The high school in the higher socioeconomic area had a higher loss rate (3.5 percent) than the school in the lower socioeconomic area (1.5 percent).[36]

Two points should be stressed from this study. First, the reported loss rate was cumulative; that is, it was not the annual loss but rather the total of missing books at the time of the study. Second, do the higher losses in the socially higher class area indicate a solid relationship between book theft and social class? Most other crimes tend to vary inversely with socioeconomic status. Perhaps book theft is more affected by the importance and frequency of book use in the daily routine. To the extent that books generally may be used and valued more by those in higher social classes, they also may be stolen more often. (This proposition is discussed further when we examine data from the national survey of crime in public libraries, Chapter 5.)

A more comprehensive study in the late 1970s found similar book losses. Yet, according to Paris, who studied the full range of public and private school libraries in Texas: "The loss and theft statistics resulting from this study are extremely low and do not substantiate the findings reported in investigations made in other parts of the nation." Paris was reacting to a 1977 survey of high school libraries on Long Island, New York, which reported annual losses as high as 32 percent![37] Certainly, in comparison, the losses in Texas schools were low. Based on a return of 48 surveys from a sample of 100, approximately 75 percent of the respondents reported 1978–1979 school year losses of less than 1 percent. Only 12.5 percent had losses of 2 percent or more. No libraries had losses exceeding 3.4 percent of the collection. In fact, these loss rates were lower than the previous year's losses; protective measures instituted during the year may have lowered the loss rate.

Earlier it was suggested that mutilation of materials tended to be directed against some types of books and periodicals more than others. Are there similar patterns for book thefts?

An early study by Roberts of university book thefts over a three-year period found differential losses for different LC classes. Among the highest losses were books on medicine, sociology, and military science. Among the lowest were volumes dealing with political science and English literature. Theft rates ranged from less than 1 percent for political science to over 2 percent for medicine.[38] Souter's research on British academic libraries described a wider range of favored targets overall, but some similar patterns within the academic fields:

> With regard to theft, examination of the literature on this point gives several strong indications. Firstly, fictional writing of all kinds is likely to be stolen; French fiction, the works of Poe and Shakespeare, and literature in general are all mentioned. Secondly, books relating to leisure activities are likely to be stolen; for example books on travel, sport, furniture, yoga, electronics. Thirdly, books on sensational subjects like sex, crime, and psychic phenomena tend to be stolen. Fourthly, in the strictly academic sphere, books in the social sciences are most likely to be stolen—psychology, sociology, education (especially physical education) and the social sciences in general.[39]

And Canada has its "booknappers," too, as indicated in Figure 7.

Problem Patron Behavior

According to Edward Delph, the public library is an "erotic oasis." Along with patrons using the library for conventional purposes, public libraries and others as well are used for unconventional activities. Says Delph:

Discriminating Booknapper Nailed in Canada

Darwin Yarish, 22, of Windsor, Canada, has admitted stealing some $40,000 worth of rare books from American and Canadian Libraries, according to the *Washington Post*. His activities were uncovered during a raid on his home. And among the loot was a $20,000 first edition of Walt Whitman's *Leaves of Grass*.

Naming those victimized by Yarish: the libraries of University of Detroit, Wayne State University, Detroit Institute of Technology, the University of Windsor, the University of Western Ontario at London, and the public libraries of Detroit and Windsor.

■ Figure 7 From *Library Journal*, September 1, 1971, p. 14.

"One of the populations that frequents the public library for unconventional goals is that of the homosexual public eroticist, i.e., males who engage in sex in public places such as public toilets, streets, theaters, libraries, and other such locations."[40]

Earlier it was suggested that ease of access to the library is a major factor that facilitates crime and disruption. This certainly appears to be true for those who choose the library as the setting for sexual contacts. Public access along with private locations within the library encourage the public eroticist to utilize such facilities. Public access is so intimately tied to problem patron behavior that citations in *Library Literature* for the topic of the "problem patron" refer the reader to "access."

Public sexual behavior in the library is not limited to homosexual contacts. At a gathering of New York City librarians who met to review security problems, a question was raised about what should be done when a couple was engaging in sex on a library table.

Inappropriate sexual activities are far from the only kind of problem patron behavior exhibited in the library. A wide range of behavior may be considered a problem for the staff and/or patrons. Any activity that causes damage, adds to the cost of maintaining the institution, endangers others, or embarrasses or frightens a conventional patron could be considered a problem. One of the more common complaints in the literature is that libraries are frequented by community-based or released mental patients. According to an article in *Library Journal*, many withdrawn patients may frequent the library, creating difficulties for the staff. One problem is deciding how best to interact with these troubled people. The article concerns only the schizophrenic patron, just one type encountered by library staff, and suggests that care be taken when dealing with patrons who find social interaction quite frightening.

> Authoritarian attitudes or smug superiority will push these people into withdrawal. On the other hand, a patronizing overconcern will also threaten them. People who have lived a lifetime feeling threatened are sensitive to nuances in the speech of others. They will reason our motives often before we do. Those who work with disturbed individuals have found that a matter-of-fact manner is most comfortable for all concerned. Since any social contact may be unbelievingly threatening, we must realize how hard it may be for the patron to ask for help.[41]

Attempting to foster comfortable interaction patterns with disturbed patrons can be trying for the staff. It is not easy to diagnose and respond appropriately. An alternative is to refer all potentially troubled patrons to local police or mental health agencies—a more hard-line approach to the problem. In response to such a suggestion, Vogel supports a more permissive policy.

> It was implied . . . that only the sane use the library for "legitimate" reasons and that emotionally disturbed people should be handed over to the police or referred to some local mental health agency. I think that we should carefully consider the consequences of these actions before such a radical "final solution" is implemented. Certainly in our library any attempt to enforce sanity as a criterion for use would severely deplete our clientele and adversely affect our statistics. Besides, where else can such people go? The best hotels would not suffer them in their lobbies, and commercial establishments would consider them an unwelcome distraction to their customers. In a public library they can (within certain limits) indulge their magnificent obsessions in a relatively permissive environment and exercise what tenuous hold they have on reality in a normal social situation.[42]

The basic question that comes to mind is whether this is a fair burden to place on librarians. As Vogel says, other institutions would not tolerate the problem. Should the library? Will this added pressure prove too disruptive to the work setting? The answer may in part depend on the skills of the staff members confronted with the patron. For those who seem to have the knack of interacting well with unusual patron behavior, the burden may be less severe than for the uninitiated or the uncomfortable staff member.

Such a problem, says Michael Vocino, was critical in some Massachusetts libraries, in part due to the policy of releasing mental patients into the community to facilitate their recovery. This and similar practices have become widespread. But problems can arise when the behavior of a former patient is still unconventional. Vocino describes some of the episodes presented at a workshop designed to help control problem patron behavior:

At the first session it seemed as though each staff member had at least one experience to relate to the group. These experiences ranged from the bizarre and violent to the somewhat comical: A middle-aged man who comes in with his hands tied together, all the while screaming obscenities at staff and public alike; An elderly woman who asks telephone reference questions which the staff tries to answer and she then refutes, using four letter words; A high school student who lifts statues from their exhibition stands and carries them around the reference room; A telephone reference patron who abuses the staff with obscenities because of what he terms "slow service." This man also thinks that one of the reference librarians played the lead role in the movie *The Exorcist* and repeatedly says so; A young woman who comes to the desk, breaks a pencil in two, and then throws the pieces at the librarian on duty; A man who gets furious when the evening paper is not available immediately; Or finally, a woman who after reading a news article screams in laughter and claps her hands over her head, to the chagrin of the library patrons.[43]

Similar complaints are heard in almost any major library system. For example, according to an article in the *New York Times* about the difficulties in that city's libraries:

In the library at Amsterdam Avenue and West 69th Street, thieves steal purses, wallets and briefcases from the readers and employees. In the Lincoln Center branch library, derelicts, many of them former mental patients, often frighten and disrupt readers and researchers. . . . The problems vary from branch to branch, and they come and go, generally rising in the spring and fall and tapering off in the summer and winter, officials said. . . . At the Lincoln Center library, George Mayer, the assistant librarian, said his staff had to deal with a number of former mental patients "dumped" out of state hospitals and into the community without follow-up or care. "They come in here cussing and shouting, and they can be really frightening," he said. "Some of them look as if they might be explosive, violent. I've seen people leave this library when just one of them comes in."[44]

Unusual episodes occur in libraries in smaller communities as well, although they are more likely in the major urban centers, with their greater concentration of treatment facilities. Many former patients appear to have few social ties within these urban centers and are more likely to "hang out" in public places. According to Bold, this and similar problems may be contributing to burnout among librarians. He says:

Libraries have evolved from temples for the learned elite to human service facilities. The library world's increasing concern with social issues and their related programs (e.g., "Headstart," adult library programs, vocational and educational guidance, information and referral, etc. . . . all available on a walk-in basis) has catapulted the public service librarian into a world of welfare clients, high school drop outs, mental hospital out-patients, ex-offenders, the indigent elderly, and patrons with sociopathic symptoms and problems insoluble at this level.[45]

What other major types of problem patron behavior affect libraries? One increasing concern is the use and sale of drugs in and around the library. The article "In New York: Reading Between the Lions" (Figure 8) provides a graphic description of some of these problems.

Once again, drug problems are not limited to the nation's largest libraries. One library director in a New England city of some 50,000 people said that youths were congregating outside the building, smoking pot and harassing patrons. In addition, drug dealers were closing transactions in isolated areas of the library or using the bathrooms as dropoff points for drugs and cash payments. This description bears a striking similarity to one from a New York City branch: ". . . about 10 young men have been gathering regularly on the library steps, 'drinking beer, smoking pot, harassing people as they come and go, particularly females.' " She added, "Think of how young girls must feel having to walk through that to use the library."[46]

Harassment of women, both patrons and staff, is a recurring problem involving direct contact as well as abusive phone calls.

> Obscene phone calls used to be a bad problem at Brooklyn Public Library. We visited Mr. John Delaney, Chief of Security at Brooklyn Public, and found out that several years ago, staff librarians adhered to the friendly but unfortunate custom of wearing name tags on their outside lapels. "People used to call up librarians using the pay phones right in the library itself," noted Mr. Delaney, "and so we finally advised the discontinuance of name tags. This pretty much solved the problem." Administrators in both large public libraries and academic libraries open to the public should take note of this tip. "In addition," noted Mr. Delaney, "we ask our librarians never to use their personal names when answering the phone. Just saying library when picking up the phone helps us to avoid many of these problems."[47]

Harassment is not limited to obscene phone calls. More subtle types of verbal abuse are frequent. Vogel relates the story of Jose, who apparently was selective in his verbal harassment. She says: "One of our most memorable patrons was Jose," who on occasion "tooted" a small brass horn in the library. But his main objective was "to find a woman," says Vogel, "an unfortunate predilection that resulted in his ultimate eviction from the premises. . . . The women who objected to his behavior were . . . the ones he informed (in no uncertain terms) . . . were not quite up to his standards."[48]

Not surprisingly, the problem of burnout, once restricted to social workers, teachers, and other service professionals, now is thought to affect public librarians as well. In his discussion of the sources of burnout among librarians, Bold says:

> Librarians work with people who use libraries for a variety of reasons. The average patron comes for books or information, and on occasion either may not be available. . . . Readers of best sellers are especially apt to confront librarians with complaints regarding the long wait for popular items, and accusations of favoritism are common. Disputes with patrons over fines, unreturned and damaged material and the like also take their toll, even though the librarian is expected to remain outwardly calm. Los Angeles library workers have one of the highest sick-time rates (when compared with other municipal workers) according to Ann Gagni, a library union officer. The record for stressful public relations must belong to a library director from New York's Long Island, who, in the course of a two-week period, lost a lawsuit brought by a library patron charging that the library didn't use due process when it revoked her library card after she refused to pay for a film damaged while in her possession and then was sued for $6,000,000 by another patron who had been banned from the library after he was caught allegedly vandalizing cars in the library's parking lot.[49]

The continuous pressures contributing to burnout were described by a participant in a workshop on the troublesome patron.

> Branch Librarian Judith Brill of New York Public's Hamilton Fish Park Branch put the problem in the perspective of a floor librarian: "We are being asked to deal with problems that have nothing to do with our training. . . . How far is our compassion supposed to go? . . . How much damage can we do without training?" Librarians, she complained, have to deal with demands from lonely old people who "monopolize library time." They must cope with complaints from regular patrons when vagrants and "bag people" invade libraries. Brill cautioned that it's sometimes dangerous to establish personal ties with people who are mentally ill, noting that Hamilton Fish had a "siege situation" to deal with when a manic-depressive turned on staffers.[50]

One of the difficulties in trying to control disruptive patron behavior is that the variety of potentially disruptive acts is enormous. These patterns of disruption often reflect what is going on in the community around the library. If, for example, drug use is a problem in the area, the possibility of drug problems in the library is increased. If vandalism is rampant, the library is more likely to be vandalized. In the mid-1970s, many public institutions witnessed acts of "streaking." This was particularly noticeable on and around college campuses. However, these acts tend to spill over into other settings as well.

> The streaking business is getting a lot tougher: a few racers have been captured by security people; at least one legislature (North Carolina) has in

■ Figure 8 From *Time Magazine,* October 8, 1979, p. 18.

In New York: Reading Between the Lions
By David Aikman

It is high noon. On the 42nd Street sidewalk outside Bryant Park two street musicians, both senior citizens, are plonking out "golden oldies" on electric guitar and zither. A few steps farther on a middle-aged black man sits on a wire wastepaper basket clutching a tattered *Reader's Digest.* He greets all passers-by with a cheery *"Auf Wiedersehen!"* But as Bryant Park comes to an end voices begin to hiss. "Wanna smoke, wanna smoke?"—twice, three, four times before a resolute reader reaches the top of the library steps and walks the hundred or so yards toward the marble lions guarding the columned portico. Along the way stands Tyrone, nineteenish, from uptown, calmly rolling his $1-apiece joints on a stone bench that he shares with a sleeping derelict. At least five pushers are holding up their plastic bags with marijuana and hashish for sale, and some customers light up on the spot. "The police used to raid early in the summer," explains Tyrone, "but you can get out in a couple of hours." He means be back on the terrace making sales, or in Bryant Park behind the building, where the pushers are so thick on the ground it takes a certain patience to refuse solicitations politely. Don't bother calling the police, either. Chances are the pusher will just plea-bargain the charge down to a $25 fine and a slight scratch on his record.

It is an average sunny lunchtime in fall at the New York Public Library. The great Central Building occupies two entire blocks of Fifth Avenue below 42nd Street. Its marble lions gaze out with dignity over trash and traffic alike, and the lofty portico proclaims the institution's origins in the heady days of 19th century hope and public benefice. "For the advancement of useful knowledge ... dedicated to history, literature and the fine arts," the letters carved in stone declare. Inside, on 88 miles of shelves, is the greatest free collection of knowledge anywhere, and on any terms one of the five outstanding libraries in the world.

Just to walk through the marble corridors and briefly visit the different specialized divisions takes an hour. The Jewish collection contains the oldest known Hebrew printed book in the world, the *Arba Turim* (four columns) from Italy. Its librarians also possess a humdinger recipe for bagels that they gladly supplied by phone to a New York baker a few years ago when he called to ask. The Main Reading Room will produce, often in less than ten minutes, the most obscure tome requested, from Milton's *Areopagitica* to Sir Richard Burton's travels in Zanzibar. For sheer accessibility nothing like it exists in any major library in the world. The service is completely free. It requires no card, no previous reference and no identification of any kind. That means, in America these days, that many rooms are plagued by the idle, the vicious, the criminal—and the literally unwashed.

"I make arrests every day," says Robert Quarg, a wiry peace officer whom the library authorities, with due literary grandiloquence, describe as the "principal bibliographic investigator." Quarg's turf is the whole library, all 5.5 million books, not to mention the 12 million prints, musical recordings, photographs and other documents housed by the N.Y.P.L.'s four research library buildings in Manhattan. Most of his time, though, is spent in the Central Building checking up on the reading rooms, corridors and special collections. "There's always something going on," he says. "One fellow stole books on chess. He left the building, went into a nearby peep-show house. I followed him there. I waited an hour inside the place for him to come out of the booth and finally I got him."

Quarg's "arrests" seldom reach court. Even if they do, the usual consequence is a $25 fine and a 15-day suspended sentence. Book thieves, in fact, are rarely caught and practically never go to jail. The security checks at the library's doors tend to be perfunctory. Strict legality favors the brazen. Due to fear of lawsuits for harassment, the library's hands are virtually tied. Guards have no legal right, for instance, to inspect women's purses less than eight inches long or to ask for explanations of suspicious-looking bulges under coat jackets. Besides, as Quarg notes, most of the book losses come through "mutilation." The thief simply rips out of a book a particular page or set of pages he finds useful or thinks he can sell. Everything is vulnerable, from telephone books to rare photographs. "Lawyers, businessmen, artists, actors, school principals—we've caught them all," says Quarg sadly. "That used to be our stamp collection," a library official remarks, pointing to a former display area. "All burglarized." Also stolen, but recovered: Norman Rockwell *Saturday Evening Post* covers from 1916 to 1969, and a small fortune in baseball cards housed in the Spalding collection. The baseball card thief was caught when a guard saw him slipping the cards into a bubble gum box taped to his briefcase. He had $5,500 in cash on him as well as a cache of smiling infielders. Richard W. Couper, 56, president and chief executive officer of the N.Y.P.L. since 1971, is blunt about the reason for the ripoffs. "This is part of the amoral society," he explains coolly. "The swipers here know what they are doing." Couper adds: "We don't even have enough money to inventory the materials."

Or to keep the library open very much. The Central Building is now closed altogether on Thursdays, and the research libraries operate only 49 hours a week, sharply down from the 1970 figure of 78 hours. The problem is that the library, despite its name, is "public" in only one aspect: its availability to the multitudes. Only $2.5 million of its annual budget is contributed by the taxpayers of New York City. The other $17.5 million comes from private bequests, state and federal grants and donations from the public. It is woefully inadequate. Priceless books are disintegrating in the humidity because there is no air conditioning. A backlog of 200,000 acquisitions in storage may take two decades to process fully. There are only 19 guards for five stories of two block-lengths each. Says veteran Library Official Walter Zervas: "If ever there was a treasure house that's going to wrack and ruin, it's this one."

For the 613,000 students, scholars, workers and dilettantes who plunge into the institution's collections each year, there are plenty of shocks and threats. Tramps are sometimes to be found stripped naked in the men's room, washing their only set of clothes. This May a reader in the Main Reading Room was suddenly stabbed by the person sitting next to him. The assailant turned out to be a mental patient on day release from a Manhattan psychiatric institution. He wanted to be readmitted because the food was better there than at home, and resorted to violence to get attention. Especially in winter, platoons of tramps drift in from the neighborhood to sleep at the tables or mutter away at readers. Periodically the library staff wakens them, with a touching politeness, and asks them to leave—or come back only after taking a bath.

Signs in the reading room warn: "Please watch your wallets, purses, and other personal possessions." Readers are not warned about the sexual perverts who, a few times each month, harass women readers. There are the "mirror guys," men with pop-down mirrors on canes that they slide under reading-room tables, the flashers and the touchers. There have even been obscene phone call experts who memorize the numbers of adjacent phone booths in the halls and ring up when a woman enters. Such incidents are often not reported. Comments veteran Library Security Officer Sivert Olenius: "We can't do a thing unless the person presses charges." Hardly anybody has the time, or the stomach, to do so.

Petty theft, book mutilation and other outrages, to be sure, have now come to seem somehow integral to the very notion of "public" in the mind of most library users. But the prevailing mood is still one of gratitude. A few days ago, Sidney Carroll, 66, a television writer and a library addict, leaned back from his notes on the turn-of-the-century Arms Tycoon Basil Zaharoff and reflected aloud: "One of the reasons I live in New York is this library. I love this room. It's hot, but not too much. The types outside the library have changed, but the caliber inside doesn't."

"Access," says President Couper, "is the name of the game. We probably do more here by way of public service than any other institution." Yet even if he had forgotten this, an inscription in the marble of Astor Hall, the library's main, high-ceilinged lobby, reminds visitors that the city of New York built the place in 1911 "for the free use of all the people." On New York's 42nd Street, that promise is all too literally being kept.

■ Figure 8 From *Time Magazine,* October 8, 1979, p. 18.

committee a bill which would make streaking at public schools and state supported institutions illegal. . . . Library scoreboard: Security guards at the Lyndon Baines Johnson library nabbed one streaker during ceremonies honoring newscaster Walter Cronkite. Another streaker announced his presence at the County of Los Angeles Public Library's reference desk, raced around the stacks, and then made a quick exit. The Lima Public Library in Ohio also had a couple of sprinters, who made their escape through a back door to a waiting car.[51]

Encouraging the staff to be aware of problems in the surrounding community as well as in the library can help to prevent or reduce those potentially disruptive episodes.

Arson

In Chapter 1 we noted that arson has been added to the F.B.I.'s list of major crimes, and it has been suggested that arson is one of the fastest growing crimes in the country. The cost of damage from arson is almost incalculable. Public institutions are frequent targets of the arsonist. Fortunately, sometimes the resulting damage is relatively minor:

> . . . Vandals got to the New England Deposit Library, setting its front door ablaze by forcing burning paper through the letter slot. Attendants at the nearby Harvard Stadium parking lot alerted the fire department. Fearing another assault by vandals, Assistant University Librarian for Building Planning Robert Walsh tried to get carpenters to board up the burned-out entrance, and after a six-hour wait he finally did the job himself.[52]

Even though the physical damage was slight, Walsh's actions are not unusual for the victim of a crime. "Fearing another assault" is a very significant statement. Physical damage is only part of the story. Again we see that whenever a crime occurs, there are both physical as well as psychological costs. Our reactions to the crime also must be considered as part of the costs. Fearing subsequent crimes because of one incident is a rational yet upsetting reaction. The New England Deposit Library was fortunate. Compare the costs experienced in Cambridge with those resulting from the fire at the Hollywood Regional Library (see Figure 9).

Special libraries are susceptible to arson as well. One week after opening, the Norfolk County (Massachusetts) House of Correction Library was closed by arson. Even though the damage in the library area was not extensive due to the massive walls used in the jail, reopening the facility took approximately two years. In fact, the entire prison remained closed during the lengthy process of allocating funds for repairs. These delays in making repairs to public institutions are examples of how the actual costs

> ### Hollywood Regional Library Destroyed in Arson Fire
>
> The Hollywood Regional Library in Los Angeles lost its longstanding battle with vandals when arsonists entered the building, painted the walls with graffiti, and then set a blaze that demolished the library and over three-quarters of its 90,000 volume collection. The 14 engine companies that responded to the 2:01 A.M. alarm battled the blaze for an hour and 15 minutes, but the two-story art deco building that opened April 30, 1940 could not be saved. Firemen protected a small portion of the collection by covering it with plastic sheeting, but most of the collection was lost, including a valuable theater arts collection, parts of which are irreplaceable. Other valuables destroyed included: a collection of the papers of President Thomas Jefferson; a rare set of Shakespeare plays; and a "very valuable" multiple set of Lewis and Clark chronicles.
>
> Early estimates put the cost of replacing the building alone at $1.7 million; library buildings are self insured by the city, and it will be up to Los Angeles to find the money to pay the bill. Another $103,000 will be needed to replace equipment, as well as $1.5 to $2 million for materials.
>
> Before the blaze, Hollywood had ranked as ninth in circulation among the Los Angeles Public Library's 62 branches.
>
> Response to the plight of the library was swift: the Los Angeles Library Association organized a meeting bringing together civic leaders and entertainment industry representatives to explore ways to raise some $.5 million to replace the entertainment and performing arts collection ruined in the fire. Johnny Carson has stepped forward to lead the effort.
>
> ■ Figure 9 From *Library Journal,* June 1, 1982.

of the crime incident can become exaggerated beyond the initial level of damage or loss.

Why does the arsonist strike? As is true with other crimes and other offenders, motives vary, but some appear more often than others. Kennedy claims that five major motives account for most of the known arson cases. These include: direct economic gain from insurance, economic gain from sources other than insurance, concealment of another criminal act (such as destroying records that have been tampered with), personal satisfaction or other factors in furthering some cause, and mental disorder. It would be useful to add another motive, common to many juvenile crimes—the attempt to impress others by taking risks. Although this is a source of "personal satisfaction," it should be viewed within the context of juvenile group behavior. Kennedy suggests that personal satisfaction and mental affliction are the motives most likely to be relevant for libraries. Furthermore, likely arson situations might include:

1. fires set by a self-professed "hero" who "discovers" it minutes later; 2. fires set by individuals to gain attention; 3. fires set out of revenge or spite (e.g., an individual who is angry at a librarian who told him to be quiet); 4. arson intended to strike back blindly at the "Establishment"; 5. fires set by persons who are legally insane or adjudged mentally incompetent; 6. fires started by pyromaniacs (sometimes connected with sexual deviancy).[53]

Libraries tend to be "good" targets for the arsonist. Kennedy suggests that the library provides the needed public access as well as the privacy that arsonists need to conceal their actions. Furthermore, the library contains many combustible materials that facilitate arson

In addition to the factors mentioned by Kennedy, there may be other facilitating conditions. The library may provide the appropriate symbolism for the vengeful arsonist. As was true of some episodes of juvenile crime, some arsonists may be seeking symbols of the society or public domain for their targets. If the anticipated reaction of the general public is important to the arsonist, then burning a library should elicit stronger responses than burning some other locations. The public's shock when a library is burned is similar to a church burning. Furthermore, libraries are likely to be centrally located within the community. This increases the public attention given to the fire itself. It is easier to attract the large crowds that may be rewarding to the arsonist when a building in a central location is the target (see Figure 10). (Findings in Chapter 4 suggest that many libraries lack even simple fire protection systems, which increases the likelihood of a successful attack.)

Assault

Studies of assault in libraries did not come to light during the literature search, but several cases have been described in various journals and provide useful information. Several of the most serious assault cases are recent. In February 1983, a fatal assault took place in Norfolk, Virginia. According to a statement in *American Libraries:*

> Just after the 9 P.M. closing on Wednesday, Feb. 23, the two staff members on duty were securing the Norfolk (Va.) Public Library System's Barron F. Black Branch, located in an average urban neighborhood. One of the staffers, a 19 year old shelver, found a youth in the stacks and told him he would have to leave. The youth whipped out a knife and slashed at her side; she ran toward the women's restroom. As she turned, she saw the youth confront the other staff member, 56 year old Gloria Lance. The man demanded Lance's car keys, then stabbed her. . . . "We are redoubling our security efforts," Gross [library director] said. "We have asked the city manager to assign trained guards to the main library and the branches on the evenings they are open."[54]

California School Library Torched

John Morris, loss control consultant for the University of California at Berkeley, reports a suspected arson at the library (a separate building) of the Concord High School. Reports Morris, the fire "happened... following a bingo game.... A janitor heard voices in the darkened library and sent an alarm to police; fires broke out in at least three places in the reading room. The loss was estimated at $120,000; half of the 25,000 books were burned or damaged; 6,000 items of audiovisual material and equipment were lost. An arson investigation was launched; 59 percent of our library fires have been arsons in late years."

Vandals Hit England Library

The *Australian Library News* reports how vandals managed to set fire to the largest library in Somerset County, England; they climbed onto the roof and used roof lights to set the blaze. Most of the damage was confined to the circulation desk area and part of the reference library. But part of the collection was damaged: 2,500 records and cassettes were destroyed and over 30,000 books damaged.

■ Figure 10 From *Library Journal*, April 15, 1979, p. 879.

Whether different types of or more security can prevent assaults such as these is an open question. Certainly, increased security does no harm except to the budget and perhaps our perceptions of the library. Unfortunately, many assaults are haphazard. That is, they occur because of a series of events. Trying to protect every library from every individual who under some conditions might commit a violent act is an impossible task. The isolated act of violence does not always occur in high-risk institutions. Yet those institutions that are plagued by crime problems naturally should be the first to consider personal security practices.

Occasionally the use of security or security personnel can facilitate problems. On March 5, 1983, a female security guard in the Cleveland Public Library was shot by an intruder. The shooting occurred while the library was closed. Public libraries are not the only library settings to experience personal assaults. In May 1983, the director of the University of Florida Library was shot by an apparently disgruntled former employee (see Figure 11).

As long as library employees interact with the public, they face the limited risks of any official who is in a public place. Crime is a problem throughout society—more serious in some locations than others—and American libraries are not exempt from these problems.

University of Florida Library Director Shot by Former Employee

A recently dismissed employee of the University of Florida library rushed past secretaries May 4 and shot and seriously wounded library director Gustave A. Harrer, a library official told *AL*.

According to Max Willocks, associate director for public services, the gunman then ran through library offices, firing at another intended victim, before being talked into surrendering his weapon by a student assistant.

Harrer, 58, had been taken off the critical list and was in serious condition at a campus hospital as *AL* went to press. A bullet was removed from his spinal cord, and doctors believe he will be paralyzed below the waist.

David Shelley, 47, was charged with attempted first degree murder. Willocks said that Shelley, a technical assistant at the information desk and a library employee for 19 years, had been dismissed on Feb. 3. The dismissal is under appeal to the Florida State Public Employees Commission.

Willocks gave this account of the tragedy:

Before the shooting, Shelley had phoned a secretary to find out whether Harrer, Willocks and Reference Department Chair Peter Malanchuk were in their second-floor offices. Shortly afterward, at about 10:20 A.M., Shelley barged past two secretaries, pulled a revolver from a paper bag, and fired four shots at Harrer from the doorway of his office, hitting him three times in the upper torso.

Shelley then burst into an adjacent conference room where 20 library staff members were meeting and shot at Malanchuk twice, missing him both times. Out of bullets, he returned to the reception area and confronted Willocks, telling him, "You are next." After this threat, Shelley rushed down the hall to reload his gun.

Shelley then went downstairs, where Dane DeRuiz, a student assistant in the circulation department, calmly engaged him in conversation and talked him into laying his gun on the reference desk and waiting for the police.

Harrer, an ALA life member, was director of libraries at Boston University before assuming his current post in 1968. He served on ALA Council from 1968 to 1971, and on the Association of Research Libraries Board of Directors from 1973 to 1976. He was also 1977–78 president of the Association of Caribbean University Research and Institutional Libraries.

Willocks told *AL,* "We on the staff find Dr. Harrer to be a very compassionate and concerned person, and for something like this to happen to him is so out of keeping with his personality . . . we're all very distressed."

■ Figure 11 From *American Libraries,* June 1983.

NOTES

1. *Sourcebook of Criminal Justice Statistics* (Washington, D.C.: Department of Justice, 1982).
2. *Violent School-Safe School Report to Congress* (Washington, D.C.: Department of Health, Education, and Welfare, 1979).
3. *New York Times,* December 20, 1980, p. 42.
4. *Boston Globe,* September 29, 1981, sec. 1, p. 17.
5. *Boston Globe,* January 25, 1983, sec. 1, p. 26.
6. George Hillery and Alan Lincoln, "Leisure, Freedom, and Crowd Behavior," *Journal of Leisure Research* 10(1978): 219–225.
7. Ralph Munn, "The Problems of Theft and Mutilation," *Library Journal* 60(1935): 589–592.
8. "A New Kind of Inventory," *Library Journal* 42(1917): 369–371.
9. "Frequency of Inventory," *Library Journal* 52(1927): 827–828.
10. Colin Ward, *Vandalism* (London: Architectural Press, 1973).
11. Dana Weiss, "Book Theft and Book Mutilation in a Large University Library," *College and Research Libraries* 42(July 1981), pp. 341–347.
12. Clyde Hendrick and Marjorie Murfin, "Project Library Ripoff: A Study of Periodical Mutilation in a University Library," *College and Research Libraries* 35(1974), pp. 402–411.
13. Weiss, "Book Theft."
14. Ibid.
15. G. H. Souter, "Delinquent Readers: A Study of the Problems in University Libraries," *Journal of Librarianship* 8(1976): 96–110.
16. Munn, "Problems of Theft," p. 591.
17. "Mutilation in the Young Adult Section," *Library and Archival Security* 2(1976): 5.
18. Mary Gouke and Marjorie Murfin, "Periodical Mutilation: The Insidious Disease," *Library Journal,* September 15, 1980, pp. 1795–1797.
19. Hendrick and Murfin, "Project."
20. Marjorie Murfin and Clyde Hendrick, "Ripoffs Tell Their Story: Interviews with Mutilators in a University Library," *Journal of Academic Librarianship* 1(1975): 8–12.
21. Ronald Hoppe and Edward Simmel, "Book Tearing and the Bystander in the University Library," *College and Research Libraries* 30(May 1969), pp. 247–251.
22. William L. Emerson, "The Theft and Mutilation of Books," *Library Journal* 85(1960): 208–209.
23. Lee Zimmerman "Pilfering and Mutilating Library Books," *Library Journal* 86(1961): 3437–3440.
24. "Prime Candidates for Theft or Mutilation," *Library Journal,* June 15, 1973, p. 1866.
25. Souter, "Delinquent Readers."
26. Gouke and Murfin, "Periodical Mutilation," p. 1796.
27. Hoppe and Simmel, "Book Tearing," p. 250.

28. Esther R. Meiboom, "Conversion of the Periodical Collection in a Teaching Hospital to Microform Format," *Bulletin of the Medical Library Association* 64 (1976): 36–40.
29. Munn, "Problems of Theft," p. 589.
30. Robert Culp, "Thefts, Mutilations, and Library Exhibits," *Special Libraries* 67(1976), pp. 582–584.
31. Janelle A. Paris, "School Library Theft," *Library and Archival Security*, 3(1980): 29–38.
32. Neal K. Kaske, "Moffitt Undergraduate Library Book Loss Study," *Library Security Newsletter* 2(1976): 6–7.
33. Souter, "Delinquent Readers," p. 99.
34. "Light Fingered Library Patrons Cost U.S. Taxpayers," *Library Science*, 1976; cited in *Library Journal* 104(June 1, 1979), pp. 1206–1207.
35. Powell Niland and William Kurth, "Estimating Lost Volumes in a University Library Collection," *College and Research Libraries* 37(1976): 128–136.
36. Norman Vinnes, "A Search for Meaning in Book Theft," *School Libraries* 18(Spring 1969), pp. 25–27.
37. Paris, "School Library Theft," p. 30; and Helen Flowers, "Rip Off Ranges Revealed," *American Libraries* 9(1978); 461.
38. Matt Roberts, "Guards, Turnstiles, Electronic Devices, and the Illusion of Security," *College and Research Libraries* 29(1968), pp. 259–275.
39. Souter, "Delinquent Readers," p. 100.
40. Edward W. Delph, "Preventing Public Sex in Library Settings," *Library and Archival Security* 3(1980): 17–26.
41. *Library Journal*, January 15, 1969, pp. 156–157.
42. Betty Vogel, "The Illegitimate Patron," *Wilson Library Bulletin* 51(1976): 65–66.
43. Michael Vocino, "The Library and the Problem Patron," *Wilson Library Bulletin* 50(1976): 372–373.
44. *New York Times*, July 11, 1981, sec. 1, p. 16.
45. Rudolph Bold, "Librarian Burn-out," *Library Journal*, November 1, 1982, pp. 2048–2049.
46. *New York Times*, July 1981.
47. "Obscene Phone Calls," *Library and Archival Security* 2(1976): 4.
48. Vogel, "Illegitimate Patron," p. 65.
49. Bold, "Librarian Burn-out."
50. "The Troublesome Patron: Approaches Eyed in NY," *Library Journal* 103(December 1, 1978), pp. 2371–2374.
51. "More Library Streaking: Jeers and Cheers," *Library Journal* 99(May 1, 1974), p. 1252.
52. "Fire and Flood Bulletin: New England Libraries Hit," *Library Journal* 101(January 15, 1976), p. 299.
53. John Kennedy, "Library Arson," *Library Security Newsletter* 2(1976): 1–3.
54. "Knife Wielding Youth Slays Public Library Staff Member," *American Libraries* 14, no. 4(1983): 174.

3 LIBRARY CRIME RESEARCH PROJECT

Much of the literature discussed in Chapter 2 involved either a case study of a single library or a somewhat broader study of several regional libraries. One of the major problems in assessing crime and disruption in public and other libraries has been the lack of a systematic series of studies of these patterns on a national level. The data described here were collected to help fill this void. The Library Crime Research Project is a three-year study of crime and disruption patterns in public libraries in the 50 states. It is a broad survey designed not only to assess problems of crime and disruption, but to identify many of the factors that contribute to or help control these problems.

PROCEDURE AND SAMPLE

The Library Crime Research Project was conducted in five stages. Stage one involved three separate pilot studies to develop and refine a useful survey instrument. Each revision resulted in additional and improved items on the questionnaire that was used in the subsequent stages.

Stages two to five each involved the selection of a certain number of states for study, and the procedure followed in each stage was identical. First, a sample of at least 60 public libraries was drawn for each state (with the exception of Arizona, Hawaii, Nevada, and Wyoming, which included only 30 each). The state sample was drawn from a comprehensive listing of all public libraries in the *American Library Directory*, by first tabulating the total number of public libraries, including branches, and then selecting every "nth" library; the ratio was determined by dividing the total number by 60. For example, if a state had 180 public libraries, every third library in the listing was included. In the several cases where the total for the state did not equal 60 libraries, the entire listing was used.

This systematic sampling helped to ensure that a representative list was obtained for each state. Only by studying a representative sample of the population can generalizations be made with some degree of confidence that the sample findings do indeed represent the entire population.

The Library Crime Research Project included nearly 3,000 public libraries in the five stages of the study. In each case an explanatory cover letter, the survey instrument, and a return envelope were sent to the head librarian. The actual mailings for stages two through five took place in October 1981, June and October 1982, and June 1983. Stage one, the pilot studies, was conducted between 1978 and 1980.

The final survey instrument was composed of a questionnaire (see Appendix A), covering such questions as: (1) characteristics of the library, (2) characteristics of the community in which the library was located, (3) descriptions of patrons and patron-use patterns, (4) experiences with 18 different types of crime and disruption, ranging from intentional book damage to assault and arson, (5) direct and indirect costs of crime, and (6) use of security equipment and procedures. All items were fixed-alternative questions constructed to obtain computer-ready responses. Fixed-alternative questions force the respondent to select from prearranged answer categories. The survey was designed so that the identity of the responding library would not be known unless the respondent chose to be identified. Returned surveys were coded and the data keypunched in preparation for analysis.

Some 2,920 surveys were distributed, and analyses were conducted on the 1,657 replies received by August 1983. The return rate of 57 percent is above average for mailed surveys of this type. In any survey there is some margin of error. That is, the results obtained may differ from the results that would have been found if everyone in the sample responded. If total accuracy is a crucial requirement, the results should be interpreted as representing only the sample of returned surveys. If a small degree of error is tolerable, the data on the returns are a good estimate of the sample. The sample in turn is representative of the full population of public libraries in the 50 states included in the study.

One problem with this type of sample should be noted. It was most important for this study that we obtained adequate representation of the libraries in each state. As a result, the full sample overrepresents some of the smaller states since 60 libraries per state were selected regardless of state size. Therefore, larger, urbanized states with more libraries tend to be underrepresented in the survey in terms of the proportion of libraries in the

TABLE 9

CITY SIZE OF SAMPLED LIBRARIES

Population	No. of Libraries	% of Libraries	Cumulative %
Less than 2,500	445	28.4	28.4
2,500–10,000	484	30.9	59.3
10,000–50,000	405	25.8	85.1
50,000–100,000	93	5.9	91.1
100,000–500,000	89	5.7	96.7
Over 500,000	47	3.0	99.7*

*Several responses were not usable.

sample. This bias in turn tends to underestimate the problems we are studying since the urbanized states generally have higher crime rates. The advantage of this type of sample is that we can examine each state separately and in enough detail to assess the relationship between crime patterns and other crucial variables. Information on crime patterns and the deployment of security items for each of the states is available (see Appendix B).

What does the sample look like? Several descriptive characteristics are discussed below, including city size, number of patrons served daily, annual circulation, size of staff, and neighborhood location. (Chapter 5 examines the way that these factors affect library crime.) New Hampshire and Massachusetts, two contrasting states, were used in pilot studies and, therefore, have larger subsamples than the other states. The range of returned surveys from the other states runs from 17 (out of 30) in Nevada to 48 in Virginia and 49 in Washington. The average number of usable returned surveys was 33.

Crime statistics quoted in Chapter 1 indicate that city size is one factor affecting the amount of crime. The libraries sampled were from a cross section of population areas. As shown in Table 9, data were obtained from 445 small town libraries with a population under 2,500, 47 cities with over one-half million people, and population areas of all sizes in between. Over half of the sample is from locations with less than 10,000 people and nearly 15 percent from cities with over 50,000.

Concerning average number of patrons using the library each day, the survey range is wide, from 1 to 10 patrons per day (reported by 5 percent of the sample) to over 250 patrons daily (reported by 16 percent). The most common response was in the 51–100 category, as shown in Table 10.

A good indicator of the activity level of the library is annual circulation. The sampled libraries reported a full range, from less than one thousand books to over one million per year. Combining these figures into six cate-

TABLE 10

REPORTED NUMBER OF PATRONS DAILY

No. of Patrons	No. of Libraries	% of Libraries	Cumulative %
1–10	85	5.6	5.6
11–20	155	10.2	15.9
21–30	149	9.8	25.7
31–50	256	16.9	42.6
51–100	331	21.9	64.5
101–250	293	19.4	83.9
Over 250	244	16.1	100.0

gories gives an overall view of the circulation patterns of the libraries. Data in Table 11 indicate that 9 percent of the respondents had less than 5,000 circulation; nearly as many had 6,000–10,000; 20 percent reported 11,000–25,000. The middle range included 14 percent with 26,000–49,000 and 19 percent had 50,000–99,000. The largest category was libraries circulating over 99,000 (30 percent).

Size of staff also provides a measure of the size and capabilities of the institution. Two-thirds of the libraries in the sample had less than 3 professional librarians and nearly half had 1 or none. Only 8 percent had 11 or more librarians. The number of aides, security personnel, and other staff also was measured. Just over one-half had 2 or less aides and about 15 percent had 10 or more (see Table 12). Only about 10 percent employed security staff. An employee index was developed by combining the four staff categories. The full range of employees was from no paid employees, found in less than 1 percent of the libraries, to 375 in one library. Fifty percent of the sample had 5 or less employees.

TABLE 11

REPORTED ANNUAL CIRCULATION

Circulation	No. of Libraries	% of Libraries	Cumulative %
0–5,000	131	9.0	9.0
6,000–10,000	121	8.3	17.4
11,000–25,000	269	18.5	35.9
26,000–49,000	199	13.7	49.6
50,000–99,000	293	20.2	69.8
Over 99,000	438	30.2	100.0

TABLE 12

PERCENTAGE OF LIBRARIES WITH VARIOUS NUMBERS OF EMPLOYEES

No. of Employees	Type of Employee				Employee Index
	Librarians	Aides	Security	Other	
0	4.4%	18.6%	91.5%	49.9%	.6%
1	41.7	18.9	4.7	21.4	10.9
2	19.9	15.7	1.1	8.7	13.5
3–5	18.3	20.9	1.1	8.6	25.6
6–10	8.0	11.8	1.0	4.1	20.0
11–20	4.4	8.3	.4	3.5	13.9
Over 20	3.3	5.8	.3	3.8	15.5

Characteristics of the library are not the only important factors that might affect patterns of crime and disruption. The social characteristics of the neighborhood in which the library is located could be a crucial determinant. The sample cuts across a variety of neighborhood settings. By far the largest category represented neighborhoods of small, one-family homes, followed by nonresidential areas and large one-family homes (see Table 13). Eight percent described the area as mostly apartments; less than 3 percent indicated housing projects were the most common. Neighborhood characteristics also were assessed by asking for a description of the social class of the neighborhood. Over half (59 percent) reported being in a middle-class neighborhood; 20 percent classified the area as lower-middle

TABLE 13

CHARACTERISTICS OF SURROUNDING NEIGHBORHOODS

Type of Housing	No. of Libraries	% of Libraries
Housing projects	34	2.6
Apartments	104	8.0
Duplex	21	1.6
Small houses	635	48.8
Large houses	249	19.1
Luxury apartments	8	.6
Nonresidential	277	21.3

class, and 16 percent as upper-middle class. The lower-class designation (4 percent) and upper-class label (2 percent) were used far less frequently.

Before we examine the findings of the current national survey, a look back at typical problems of the early 1970s might be of interest. A study conducted by the Burns Security Institute of 255 libraries is summarized in Figure 12. Note that the libraries sampled were primarily large facilities and that the authors and library directors had differing views of the most crucial problems.

CRIME PATTERNS

The Library Crime Research Project measured the incidence of 18 different types of crime and disruption. These problem behaviors have been classified into five categories: (1) vandalism, (2) theft, (3) problem patron behavior, (4) assault, and (5) arson.

There is a wide range in both the nature and the impact of the acts studied. Estimates of crime obtained in this study tend to be conservative, with several factors contributing to this. Initially, as noted earlier, the larger, urbanized states were somewhat underrepresented in the full sample. To the extent that these are the states with the higher crime rates, the estimates will be low. Second, the rate of return of the questionnaire was lower for the largest libraries in the sample. This means that those libraries with the greatest amount of crime were less likely to be included in the results. In addition, much crime in the library is hidden—unknown to the respondents. Furthermore, some of the crime that was not hidden might have been selectively nonreported. Several factors might influence a decision not to report crime problems in a survey, including concern that the administrator might be perceived as unable to maintain a safe and efficient institution. Other episodes might go unreported because they are not defined as crimes. For example, missing books might be labeled as long overdue rather than stolen, which would lower the estimates of crime. Finally, the survey's use of the term *episode* may have resulted in conservative estimates. An episode is an event, but the event may have involved the theft of a single volume or several hundred volumes. Counting episodes minimizes the size or magnitude of each specific occurrence.

Vandalism

Six types of vandalism were examined, including intentional book damage, vandalism both outside and inside the building, vandalism to cars of both patrons and staff, and intentional damage to equipment. (Chapter 5 analyzes the ways in which various library and community characteristics

Fire Rated Top Problem in Security Study

The Burns Security Institute in Briarcliff Manor, New York has concluded that vulnerability to fire is the biggest threat facing libraries—a judgment which runs counter to the majority opinion of some 255 public library directors who participated in the institute's recent questionnaire survey on library security. Some 215 municipal libraries, 39 county and regional libraries, and one state library supplied the input for the institute's *National Survey on Library Security,* and the majority of them said that book theft, vandalism, and nonreturn of books are their top security problems. The responding libraries reportedly make a representative cross-section with a total circulation of over 92 million volumes. The institute, however, based its contention that fire is a much more serious threat on these points: more than six out of ten reporting libraries have no fire alarms; nearly nine out of ten have no automatic sprinkler systems; and half have neither guards nor burglary or fire alarms.

Book theft was rated as the top security problem by an overwhelming majority, but most library directors could only approximate the actual extent of losses, since, in most cases, there are no current inventories. The institute, working with estimates from 140 libraries, pegged total annual losses at $437,400, or an average of $3,120 per library. Some 104 libraries sent in estimates on the loss of rare and irreplaceable books—an average of 85 books per library.

Only one out of ten officials was willing to venture an opinion on employee dishonesty, but 24 of them expressed the opinion that employees are pilfering books or being dishonest in other ways. Opinion is divided as to whether or not book theft has worsened over the past five years. The institute urged libraries to conduct periodic inventories, arguing that it would be easier to make a case to authorities and the public for funding support for more security.

Other security problems: The great majority of reporting libraries said that they have no special protection for valuable exhibits, either permanent or temporary. The institute saw as a more serious problem the lack of ability to regulate access to closed stacks

Vandalism and disorderly conduct, said the report, are considered serious problems, but the institute noted that physical assaults are "negligible," with only 41 being recorded nationwide over the past year by reporting libraries. It warned that misbehavior may "flare into something worse when the staff is unable to cope," and it noted that problems of this type can keep patrons away from the library.

Other recommendations: the report urged library directors to solicit the help of police and fire departments in surveying premises and making recommendations for effective fire and crime prevention programs. It also noted that private security firms may be willing to provide the desired surveys without charge and that local insurance advisers can also be helpful.

■ Figure 12 From *Library Journal,* October 15, 1973, p. 2954.

affect the crime patterns presented here.) Table 14 contains the basic findings for all types of problems. The most common type of vandalism was intentional book damage. Two-thirds of the sample reported at least 1 episode. Twenty-one percent were aware of 1 or 2 episodes; 18 percent reported 3–5 occurrences. Just over 10 percent had 6–10 repetitions. Over 10 cases of intentional book damage during the year were reported by 16 percent of the sample. The measure of chronic intentional book damage (6 or more cases) showed that over one-fourth of the responding libraries were in this category.

Two points should be clarified here. First, an episode of vandalism often involved more than a single volume. No attempt was made in the survey to measure how many books were involved or how valuable they were. (This would be useful to pursue in subsequent studies, but the decision was made here to focus on the number of episodes.) Second, like any crime statistics, these may be underestimated. It is likely that some respondents did not tell about disruptive episodes in their library either by choice or due to lack of awareness—"Most of these items are answered 'never' because no one has actually been caught in the act. We know it happens, but we haven't caught

TABLE 14

PERCENTAGE OF PUBLIC LIBRARIES REPORTING CRIME AND DISRUPTION

Type of Episode	Number of Episodes				
	0	1–2	3–5	6–10	Over 10
Intentional book damage	34%	21%	18%	10%	16%*
Book theft	20	14	14	13	39
Reference material stolen	37	23	18	10	13
Equipment stolen	78	16	4	1	1
Other theft	66	21	8	3	3
Vandalism outside building	46	32	13	5	4
Vandalism inside building	56	24	10	6	5
Vandalism of patrons' cars	87	9	3	1	0
Vandalism of staff cars	84	13	3	1	0
Vandalism of equipment	83	11	4	2	1
Drug use by patrons/staff	85	9	3	1	2
Drug sale by patrons/staff	96	3	1	0	0
Verbal abuse of patrons	72	16	6	3	2
Verbal abuse of staff	55	23	9	6	7
Indecent exposure	83	12	4	1	1
Assault on patrons	93	5	1	0	0
Assault on staff	97	3	1	0	0
Arson	96	4	0	0	0

*Figures may not total 100% due to rounding.

anyone." In other cases, problems like intentional book damage and book theft may have occurred, but they were not defined in those ways. They may have been labeled as less serious, such as unintentional damage or overdue and lost books. In addition, each survey was most likely completed by one employee. More episodes may have been uncovered if other employees had been questioned. Here are some responses:

> No actual thefts that we know of, but about 30 long overdue books that were probably charged out and most probably will never be returned.

> Although you do not ask for comments, I feel that one item should be explained: the large number of stolen books. Many of these, perhaps 30%, are stolen in the manner of shoplifting. The rest, some 70%, are checked out, but the borrowers do not take the trouble to return them. We have been getting warrants against these, but the police do not take the time and bother to deliver them so that a court case ensues. This is our biggest "security" problem.

> If you regard books overdue 6 months or more as theft. We do! It's a problem for us.

> We are open two days a week and our damage and loss are more the result of a lack of responsibility of parents over their children than vandalism. Broken windows by playing ball where they shouldn't be, etc., unreturned books, pages gone, general signs of the times.

> We have cases of people just keeping books they've checked out and never returning them, which is the same as stealing perhaps, but I have no record of how many stolen, only of books called lost.

Two items focused on building vandalism. Outside damage proved to be more common than vandalism inside the building. Over half of the respondents had experienced at least one act of outside vandalism. These included the common broken window and spray painting as well as destruction of book drops and doors. Nearly one-third of the libraries had one or two occurrences, and just less than 10 percent had six or more episodes.

Although somewhat less common, vandalism inside the building was still a serious problem. One-quarter of the sample reported one or two cases, and over 10 percent had chronic problems (six or more repetitions). One small town library reported: "Our problems are mainly outside—graffiti, eggs, catsup, etc. Broken windows—shot by a BB gun. Groups of middle and high [school] kids congregate on and around the building and give us fits. Just today I picked up a 6 pak of empty beer bottles." And "We get a lot of smashed liquor bottles. The drinkers park in our lot and take aim at the building." Another library commented: "Crime has cost us little, but we have had problems. Pop, beer, milk, ice cream, chocolate, anything oily (potato chips, etc.) have been dumped into the bookdrop and have damaged books."

Vandalism or intentional damage to equipment occurred in less than 20 percent of the institutions studied, and in half of these cases occurred only once or twice. Apparently since some equipment is portable, it can be more easily protected than the building itself. Only 3 percent of the sample had chronic equipment damage, which may occur less frequently than building damage, but its effects may be more far reaching. Most but not all building damage has social effects. It is offensive to observers and patrons, may increase levels of apprehension, and may even facilitate more damage through the modeling effect. Damage to equipment may cause these reactions if it is visible to the public, but it also affects the functioning of the library. That is, both function and social climate may be touched. Even if the equipment damage is not public knowledge, the staff will probably be affected by the episodes.

Theft

Cases of theft are among the most common criminal offenses in the United States. In a single year, millions of larceny-thefts may be reported to police, and many millions more are not reported. In the public library, too, theft is one of the most frequent crimes.

The Library Crime Research Project measured four kinds of theft: book, reference material, equipment, and "other" theft. Book theft was the most common offense reported. Eighty percent of the respondents indicated at least one episode. Of these cases, the majority had more than 6 episodes; 14 percent reported 1 or 2 cases, 14 percent were aware of 3–5 repetitions, and 13 percent had 6–10 cases. Over one-quarter of the sample indicated that book theft occurred more than 20 times. Once again, it should be noted that an episode often involved more than a single volume. Many respondents indicated knowing that book theft was a problem, but that they could not give accurate estimates because of inventory problems. One said: "Our book and reference material theft figures noted above are only a guess; we have never seen it happen, but lots of materials have disappeared." Or: "This library is a special library, serving [the] state government. There are no evening hours; nearly all patrons are working adults. The building is located within a complex of government buildings . . . in the central city. Theft that is most easily detected by us is the taking of books and sometimes other items—which we attribute to the night time cleaning staff—staff that change frequently . . . and [are] difficult to control!"

The second most common type was the theft of reference material. Although not as frequent as book theft, reference theft has resulted in the loss of many valuable reference sources. Nearly one-fourth of the sample reported 1 or 2 occurrences, and 18 percent had 3–5 thefts. Over one-fifth had chronic reference theft.

Theft in San Francisco

The newsletter of the San Francisco Public Library reports that an anonymous tip led the San Francisco Police Department to raid the apartment of a 55-year-old patron. Police officers recovered three large boxes filled with expensive art books that had been stolen from SFPL. And newsletter editor David Belch notes in his report of SFPL's "crime wave" that patrons will go after more than books in these modern times: "A sneak thief absconded with the piano from the Noe Valley Branch."

Nail Down Your OCLC Terminals

The Library Department of City College of New York reports that it scored a first when thieves made off with a $3700 OCLC terminal—the first to be stolen from any library since OCLC began in 1972. The thieves also stole two typewriters and a filmstrip reader.

■ Figure 13 From *Library Journal*, September 1, 1979, p. 1207.

Other studies have shown that theft of reference material causes great inconvenience in public and academic libraries. High costs are incurred and much time is spent replacing the material. Patrons in need of the material on short notice are also inconvenienced.

Another item on the survey asked about theft of equipment, a chronic problem in only 2–3 percent of the sample. However, at least one episode was uncovered in nearly one-quarter (22 percent) of the sample. Most of these cases involved one or two such episodes. Our respondents were not alone (see Figure 13).

The fourth type of theft examined involved the catch-all category of "other theft." Two-thirds of the respondents reported no "other thefts." Twenty-one percent noted one or two offenses, and about 5 percent had chronic problems. Much of this type of theft was not likely to be known by the respondents. The theft of personal property or cash may not be reported to an administrator. Said one respondent:

> The first three years in the new building we had purse snatchings, a prowler in the parking lot, and theft of library and personal possessions. Very little since then. Our book inventory in 1976 revealed only 162 books unaccounted for and presumed stolen. . . . Magazines do disappear with some regularity, but it is way too few to be concerned about.

The theft index, which examines the four theft items together, shows that only 17 percent of the respondents had no theft at all. At the other extreme, only two libraries reported being the victim of all four kinds of theft more than 20 times each.

Fear of theft certainly is a problem. The following sign was posted in a small New England public library. "This is a public library, protect your belongings." Imagine having to remind patrons that *because* it is a public library, it is necessary to guard one's possessions. These are the subtle types of problems that affect many public institutions. And although subtle, these concerns inhibit public enjoyment and possibly use of the library.

Problem Patron Behavior

The range of activities that patrons can engage in while in the library almost defies description. It is very difficult to prescribe programs to curtail the disruptive patron when one does not know what the disruptive activity will be. Based on a review of existing studies and case histories, the survey focused on verbal abuse, drug use and sale, and indecent exposure. Certainly these activities do not exhaust the list of common patron problem activities, but the selection is representative of the kinds and frequencies of disorder.

When asked about drug use by staff or patron, 15 percent of the respondents indicated knowing about it. Patron drug use was not singled out from staff drug use, and both apparently are problems in some locations.

Drug use was a chronic problem in only 3 percent of the sample. Many cases involved the same staff member or patron using the library as their favorite location to use drugs. Several respondents indicated that once the pattern was broken through intervention by staff or police, the problem diminished. This is a good example of redefining the library as an inappropriate place to engage in illegal activities. Regardless of why the library had initially been defined as an appropriate target or hangout, intervention can quickly lead to a reevaluation of its suitability for drug use.

Drug sales in the library rarely were a problem. Only 4 percent mentioned sales by staff or patrons. Almost all of those involved less than five episodes. It is important to note that drug sales are generally a most secretive criminal activity. Both parties, knowing they are engaged in an illegal act, go to great lengths to hide their involvement in most cases. The fact that these activities were observed in nearly 60 different libraries in the sample is surprising.

The second type of problem patron behavior involved what was called verbal abuse, including abuse of another patron as well as abuse of a staff member. Of the two, verbal abuse of staff was more common. Nearly half of the respondents told of at least one case of verbal abuse of a staff member. Half of these reportedly occurred once or twice. In 10 percent of the cases, verbal abuse was recognized 3–5 times and was chronic in over 13 percent of the libraries.

> Special note: Most of our problems have been with drunks . . . that have been sleeping in the rear parking lot of our library. We are located next to a large grocery store and the drunks purchase/steal liquor from there and drink it on our property. The winos panhandle our patrons outside and occasionally enter and bother the staff. The police are called immediately once we determine there are drunks in or around the library. Police are called at least 8–10 times a month. . . . We are located two blocks from a major highway—reason for so large a number of drunks.

> We are located in a very low crime area of rural Texas. About all we experience are people with unusual views of reality and dogs.

Recording verbal abuse of a patron is more difficult since the patron who is exposed to the abuse may not mention it to anyone who might report it. Even so, more than one-fourth of the returns mentioned verbal abuse of a patron. Usually this occurred only once or twice, but it was chronic in 5 percent of the sample. What constitutes verbal abuse varies. In some locations, comments that are met with outrage and shock by patrons would be ignored by patrons in other settings, probably because they are more commonplace.

> In response to your questionnaire, we are happy to report that in our small logging community of 1,800, in the backwoods of northern Idaho, we are virtually free of the problems listed. Would say that crime and violence have no effect on our services to the public. The "verbal abuse" comes from patrons who have moved here to escape from all the urban problems, then can't understand why we don't have all the facilities of a big city library.

> Please note: We are a special case because we are a public library and a high school library located inside a high school. Therefore we have more patron abuse of other patrons, occasional fights, etc., mainly during the school year. Our adults during the evening hours are pretty tame.

The final measure of problem patron behavior assessed incidents of indecent exposure. The term was not defined in the questionnaire and, therefore, the answers may include a range of actual incidents. With this in mind, nearly 20 percent of the sample indicated awareness of at least one incident. Usually this involved only one or two episodes. In fact, indecent exposure was a chronic problem in less than 2 percent of the responding libraries. Examination of the problem patron index indicates that 52 percent of the sample experienced at least one episode.

You do not mention the presence in libraries of mentally disturbed people. They do some fairly strange things. The policy of "asylums" to dismiss patients who are still disturbed and under medication can make a problem in small communities. But people like that have to have some haven too. I just hide the big art books when I see them coming.

Assault

The most frightening crime that can occur in the library or any other public institution involves violence. Among the most common types of violent crime are assaults, which fortunately are not common against staff and patrons. Of the two, assaults against staff members were reported to be less frequent than similar assaults against patrons. Only 7 percent of the sample reported an assault against a patron while in the library or on library grounds. The vast majority of these occurred only once or twice. Less than 2 percent indicated three or more episodes. Similar patterns were found for assaults against a staff member. Three percent of the respondents indicated knowledge of an assault against a staff member. Less than 1 percent reported three or more assaults. If the two assault items are combined, nearly 8 percent of the sample knew of one assault or more. Only 3 percent had multiple episodes. Said one respondent: "One employee was threatened with a 22 calibre pistol if she did not have sex with him—he has psychological and mental problems." And: "The older people seem to have some problems. One of them was roughed up when someone tried to take her purse."

Arson

From the perspective of managing an institution, arson is perhaps the most devastating crime that can occur. In fact, the Burns Security Institute study conducted in the early 1970s listed arson as the greatest threat to libraries (see Figure 12). Many incidents of arson are relatively minor, either because they are detected early or not expertly set. Occasionally arson totally destroys the institution. Data show that 4 percent of the responding libraries experienced at least one episode of arson during the year in question. Several others reported fires that were not considered suspicious. Only ten of the total sample reported more than one episode.

Total Index

A good measure of the crime activity affecting libraries is the total index calculated by including any episode of crime or disruption that may have occurred. Eleven percent of the sample claimed to be free from all the types of crime and disruption that were investigated. This index totals the scores for each of the 18 items (see Table 14). The scores ranged from 0 to

6 for each item, with 6 indicating "over 20 times." On this scale, 10 percent of the sample had scores of 30 or more. The range was 0–72, with a mean of 13.

HIGH- AND LOW-CRIME LIBRARIES

What does the average library experience during the year in terms of crime? According to the survey, for the 12-month period assessed, the average library had just over two episodes of intentional book damage and four cases of book theft. Reference material was stolen twice a year, and equipment was stolen less than once a year. Vandalism outside the building occurred slightly more than once a year, as did vandalism inside the building. Damage to cars owned by staff or patrons and damage to library equipment typically occurred less than once a year.

The average library also had less than one episode of drug sale or use in the library and probably no assaults or arson. Verbal abuse of staff or patron each occurred once, and indecent exposure occurred less than once a year. These typical occurrences should not be confused with the range of episodes. Many libraries as we have shown had chronic problems throughout the year; others had virtually no disruptive events.

The High-Crime Library

The term *high-crime library* refers to those facilities with total crime index scores in the top 10 percent of the sample. This subsample had scores of at least 30 on the index, which was the summation of the 18 different crime and disruption problems.

TABLE 15

CHARACTERISTICS OF SAMPLED LIBRARIES

Characteristic	Low-Crime Libraries	High-Crime Libraries
City size estimate	less than 2,500	40,000–50,000
Number of patrons daily	20–25	250+
Annual circulation	6,000–10,000	100,000+
Number of employed librarians	1	4–5
Number of employed aides	0–1	6–10
Number of employed security personnel	0	0–1
Total employees	1–2	30–35
% in middle-class neighborhoods	62%	39%

TABLE 16

PERCENTAGE OF HIGH-CRIME PUBLIC LIBRARIES REPORTING CRIME AND DISRUPTION

Type of Episode	Number of Episodes				
	0	1–2	3–4	6–10	Over 10
Intentional book damage	2%	4%	15%	18%	61%
Book theft	0	1	5	2	92
Reference material stolen	5	4	26	19	47
Equipment stolen	35	41	14	2	7
Other theft	19	36	25	12	8
Vandalism outside building	7	18	38	21	17
Vandalism inside building	7	21	22	24	27
Vandalism of patrons' cars	49	27	15	4	5
Vandalism of staff cars	41	44	9	5	1
Vandalism of equipment	24	38	21	12	6
Drug use by patrons/staff	52	21	12	7	8
Drug sale by patrons/staff	81	11	2	2	4
Verbal abuse of patrons	26	25	22	18	9
Verbal abuse of staff	5	15	28	20	32
Indecent exposure	41	35	18	4	2
Assault on patrons	78	20	1	1	0
Assault on staff	88	9	2	0	0
Arson	88	11	1	0	0

Summary	% with 1 or More Episodes
Theft	98
Vandalism	99
Drug use/sale	57
Verbal abuse	95
Assault	27
Total	99

What can we tell about the typical library experiencing the highest crime rate? How does it compare with the average or low-crime library? (See Table 15.) The crime rate in the high-crime sample was significantly greater than in the full sample. These differences can be seen by comparing Tables 14 and 16. Briefly, it was typical for these libraries to have chronic problems with book damage, book and reference material theft, vandalism, and verbal abuse of staff. Even the uncommon crimes occurred relatively frequently. For example, over half of the high-crime libraries experienced vandalism of staff and patrons' cars, and nearly one-fourth noted assaults against patrons. Arson and assaults on staff were reported by 12 percent of this group.

The crime index shows that nearly all of these libraries experienced some type of theft, vandalism, and verbal abuse; over half knew of drug use or sales. Just over one-quarter had some type of assault on the premises. Many of the differences between the high- and low-crime libraries are consistent with the literature on the factors affecting crime.

As shown in Table 15, the typical high-crime library in the survey was located in a city of nearly 50,000 people. Only 1 percent was in towns of less than 10,000 people. The activity level of the library was measured by patron-use and circulation figures. Over half of this subsample had more than 250 patrons daily, and only 5 percent had less than 50 patrons daily. Circulation was also brisk. Three-quarters of this group had a circulation of 100,000 per year or more, and all had circulated at least 10,000 volumes during the year.

High-crime libraries also were characterized by larger staff size. For example, there were more than 4 professional librarians per library, with one-fourth of the sample employing over 10 professionals. These libraries also were more likely to employ 1 or more security personnel (25 percent). One-half of these libraries had 25 or more employees in all. Total employees ranged from 1 to 287.

When asked to describe the social class of the surrounding neighborhood, the most common response was middle class (39 percent) followed by lower-middle class (32 percent). Only 8 percent described the area as lower class. Nearly half of the high-crime libraries (48 percent) were located in neighborhoods with small, one-family homes, and 22 percent were located in nonresidential areas.

The Low-Crime Library

How do low-crime libraries compare with high-crime libraries on the same characteristics? There were major differences on most but not all indicators (see Table 15). Ninety-five percent of the libraries reporting no episodes of crime or disruption were in towns with populations under 10,000.

The immediate location of the library was described as middle class (62 percent) or as upper-middle class (16 percent). Only 2 percent was in locations described as lower class. Forty percent of the neighborhoods contained small one-family homes; over one-fourth had large one-family houses. Similar to the high-crime libraries, nearly one-fourth were located in nonresidential areas.

As expected, the activity level of low-crime libraries was substantially lower than the high-crime libraries. Nearly half (48 percent) served less than 20 patrons a day, and only 8 percent averaged more than 50 patrons daily. Over one-third (35 percent) had annual circulations below 5,000, and half had less than 10,000 volumes circulating. Only 4 percent circulated more than 50,000 items. Nearly three-quarters were located in small towns with fewer than 2,000 people.

Staff size also differentiated the two types of institutions. Over three-quarters of this group had either no professional librarians (8 percent) or only one professional (69 percent). Only one library had security personnel. The range of total employees was from 1 (37 percent) to 42 (1 percent). Only 10 percent of the sample had more than 4 employees.

REGIONAL PATTERNS

The statistics collected annually by the Justice Department and other measures of crime show that different geographic regions of the country often exhibit different crime patterns. In Chapter 1 we noted that crime in general was highest in the West and lowest in the Midwest. In addition, patterns of specific major crimes often varied from region to region.

Do these same trends hold when examining crime in the library? The survey sample allows us to duplicate the regions identified by the Justice Department for the purposes of comparing crime rates—the Northeast, the South, the Midwest or north central area, and the West. As did the *Uniform Crime Reports,* the survey found differences in crime patterns for the different regions. These differences included both an overall variation in the amount of crime in libraries as well as differences within the specific categories of crime (see Table 17). Examination of the total index shows that the southern states in the sample had the highest frequency of reported offenses; the north central region had the lowest.

When considering patterns in the South, we find that the rate is not uniformly high. In particular, problems of book damage and book theft were higher in the South than in any other region. Table 17 shows the average crime scores for each type of crime and disruption. The possible scores range from 0 to 3, with 3 indicating 3–5 episodes per year, 4 (6–10 episodes), 5 (11–20 episodes), and 6, over 20 episodes per year. Several other types of crime and disruption were highest in the South, including "other thefts," drug use by staff or patron, verbal abuse of staff, and indecent exposure.

The northeastern region had the highest scores on several items, including theft of reference material and equipment and all five vandalism indicators. The sampled western states typically fell in the middle to low ranges of crime, and the north central states were lowest on all items except "other theft."

TABLE 17

AVERAGE PUBLIC LIBRARY CRIME SCORES BY REGION

Type of Episode	Region			
	Northeast	South	North Central	West
Intentional book damage	1.9	2.4	1.9	2.0
Book theft	3.4	3.6	3.0	3.4
Reference material stolen	2.5	2.1	1.6	1.8
Equipment stolen	.6	.5	.4	.4
Other theft	.7	.8	.7	.6
Vandalism outside building	1.5	1.2	1.0	1.1
Vandalism inside building	1.4	1.2	.9	1.0
Vandalism of patrons' cars	.3	.3	.2	.2
Vandalism of staff cars	.4	.3	.2	.2
Vandalism of equipment	.5	.4	.3	.3
Drug use by patrons/staff	.4	.5	.3	.4
Drug sale by patrons/staff	.1	.1	.1	.1
Verbal abuse of patrons	.7	.7	.5	.5
Verbal abuse of staff	1.2	1.3	.9	1.1
Indecent exposure	.3	.5	.2	.2
Assault on patrons	.1	.1	.1	.1
Assault on staff	.1	.1	.03	.02
Arson	.04	.1	.1	.03
Summary				
Theft	6.7	6.8	5.4	6.1
Vandalism	6.5	5.5	4.4	4.9
Drug use/sale	.4	.5	.4	.5
Verbal abuse	2.0	2.0	1.4	1.6
Assault	.2	.1	.1	.1
Total	13.8	14.2	11.3	12.8

Regional patterns for the different occurrences also were examined by computing the percentage of libraries reporting at least one occurrence of the act in question (see Table 18). With this measure, we noted patterns similar to those indicated by the average crime scores. This specific measure does not take into account patterns of repetition or chronic crime, but rather tells the proportion of libraries that are affected to any degree. Once again, libraries in the South reported the greatest amounts of overall crime and disruption. Theft was most widespread in southern libraries, and acts of vandalism were most often seen in the Northeast. The north central region again appears to have the least significant problem with crime.

TABLE 18

PERCENTAGE OF REGIONAL PUBLIC LIBRARIES REPORTING AT LEAST ONE DISRUPTIVE EPISODE FOR A 12-MONTH PERIOD

Type of Episode	Northeast	South	North Central	West
Intentional book damage	60%	73%	60%	66%
Book theft	79	82	75	82
Reference material stolen	73	67	53	62
Equipment stolen	27	25	18	22
Other theft	29	39	28	30
Vandalism outside building	57	56	48	53
Vandalism inside building	50	50	36	41
Vandalism of patrons' cars	16	14	9	12
Vandalism of staff cars	20	17	13	16
Vandalism of equipment	23	16	16	14
Drug use by patrons/staff	15	20	10	15
Drug sale by patrons/staff	2	4	5	3
Verbal abuse of patrons	26	30	23	24
Verbal abuse of staff	41	48	39	45
Indecent exposure	17	25	13	15
Assault on patrons	8	6	3	7
Assault on staff	4	4	2	2
Arson	4	5	4	3

PERSONAL VICTIMIZATION

Several items on the survey instrument asked for personal information about the respondent. In this way we hoped to obtain some idea of the characteristics of those who completed the survey. Whether the respondent is typical of others on the library staff is not clear. The questions asking for this personal information were described as voluntary.

Approximately 65 percent of the returned surveys did contain the personal responses. Based on these returns, the respondents were typically female, head librarians, and over the age of 40. Specifically, 75 percent of the identified respondents were women and 82 percent of the returns were completed by the head librarian. Just over half of the respondents were over the age of 40, with another 37 percent between 25 and 40.

In response to the question about whether the respondent was ever the victim of a crime in the library, nearly 80 percent indicated "never." The majority of the remaining victimized librarians had experienced only one such incident; 6 percent had been victims more than once.

86 □ CRIME IN THE LIBRARY

Patterns of victimization were examined to see if the sex of the respondent was related to the likelihood of being a victim in the library. As might be expected based on national crime data, men had higher victimization scores than did the women who responded. In fact, the victimization rate was twice as high for the men in the sample. For the male respondents, over 20 percent were victimized once; another 12 percent were victims of crime twice or more. In comparison only 18 percent of the female respondents were victimized while at the library. The majority of the female victims suffered one episode; only 5 percent were victimized two or more times.

Apparently patterns of victimization within the library setting are not unlike those in other areas. Earlier we noted that in general males were more likely to become victims than were females. Within the library setting, some might expect that women would be more likely to be singled out for offenses, but this does not appear to be so. The seriousness and impact of these offenses on the victim were not assessed. It is possible that male and female employees were victims of different types of crimes.

TRENDS OVER TIME

During the final stage of sampling (June 1983), the two states used in the pilot studies were re-examined. New Hampshire was first studied in 1978 and again in 1983. The first data were collected from Massachusetts in 1980, resulting in a three-year gap. Not all of the current questions had

TABLE 19

AVERAGE CRIME/DISRUPTION SCORES FOR NEW HAMPSHIRE/MASSACHUSETTS LIBRARIES

Type of Episode	NH 1978	NH 1983	MA 1980	MA 1983
Book damage	1.1	.9	2.9	2.9
Vandalism outside building	.6	.9	2.6	1.8
Vandalism inside building	.5	.6	2.5	1.7
Vandalism of patrons' cars	NR*	.1	.7	.3
Vandalism of staff cars	NR	.2	.9	.6
Vandalism of equipment	.4	.3	1.2	.8
Verbal abuse of patrons	NR	.3	1.1	.5
Verbal abuse of staff	.7	.5	1.7	1.1
Assault on patrons	NR	0.0	.3	.1

*NR = not recorded.

been included in the pilot studies. However, 6 items for New Hampshire and 11 for Massachusetts can be compared.

There were slight differences in sampling the pilot states and the other 48. The original New Hampshire study included all libraries in towns with populations exceeding 1,000. The second run sampled 60 libraries from all cities, including those with a population less than 1,000. This difference would tend to deflate the rate of crime in the newer sample. The Massachusetts pilot had 100 systematically selected libraries, but branch libraries were not represented in proportion to their numbers. In the current survey, the branch libraries had an equal chance of being selected as the largest libraries in the state. Therefore, there are more branches in the second sample, which also would tend to lower some of the average crime scores.

Do any trends across time appear between the two studies? Overall, New Hampshire has slight increases in vandalism of the building, but slight decreases in book damage and verbal abuse of staff. Keep in mind that New Hampshire had and still has relatively low rates of crime and disruption. In contrast, Massachusetts has relatively high rates of library problems, but these appear to have decreased since 1980. All of the items being compared show lower average scores in 1983 than in 1980. As can be seen in Table 19, there are marked decreases in types of vandalism as well as in assaults and verbal abuse. Some of the decrease is due to the presence of more small branches in the second sample. However, when these branches are excluded, there is still some decrease in types of crime and disruption. The decrease also appears related to wider use of some security measures in Massachusetts libraries. (This possibility is discussed in greater detail in Chapter 4.)

4 THE IMPACT OF CRIME

As crime in the United States has become a more significant problem, a relatively new focus in its study has developed. Along with the traditional concerns about crime patterns, causes, and characteristics of the offender, an emphasis on the crime victim has gained in importance. This focus has grown into a social science specialty known as victimology.

How is victimology distinguished from the more traditional concerns of criminology? The first major difference is that criminologists tend to emphasize the criminal or the offender. The more that the criminologist can discover about the characteristics of offenders, the easier it may be to predict and control crime. Typical areas of attention include the study of characteristics such as age, sex, social class, racial or ethnic origin, residence patterns, and so on. Earlier we discussed several broad categories of crime theory, including biological, psychological, and social explanations. These are the same kinds of emphases that criminologists may adopt when studying the offender. Psychological factors, including personality traits, motives and needs, or biological states such as genetic makeup, physical disorders, or nutritional patterns, might be emphasized. Other criminologists may choose to stress some combination of biological, social, or psychological factors. That is, the importance of the family as it relates to personality formation may be emphasized. In any case, the focus is on the offender and his or her behavior.

Obviously, the concerns of the victimologist would be different. The emphasis here might be on the physical, social, or psychological characteristics of the victim. The goal of such studies would be to determine the importance of the victim's age, sex, or physical condition. Examination has shown life-style and habits to be important determinants of victimization patterns. Where people live as well as their socioeconomic class are related to the possibility of becoming victims. Psychological traits have been examined as possible factors. Even though the criminologist emphasizes the offender and the victimologist focuses on the victim, the specific conditions that each examines in his or her subject are similar.

A second difference is that criminologists usually focus on the causes of crime; the victimologist questions the causes of being victimized. For example, some researchers ask "Why do crime rates vary?" and others may ask "Why do rates of victimization vary?" Similarly we could focus on why some people become offenders or why some people become victims. A third difference in orientation involves examining the effects of the criminal justice system on offenders and the effects of victimization on the life and career of the victim.

Another difference is seen in the attention paid to the impact of crime (victimology) and the type or pattern of crime (criminology). Even though the two are not independent of each other, they often are studied separately. Criminologists might be more interested in the rates, types, patterns, increases and decreases in crime, and the factors that influence each of these. A victimologist might be more interested in the impact of these crime patterns on victims and potential victims. Victims, of course, could be individuals, families, groups, or institutions such as schools and libraries.

The impact of crime is not easy to assess. One way is to adopt Conklin's approach to the study of the costs of crime.[1] This involves examining both the direct and indirect costs of crime. Whenever someone or some facility is victimized, costs are incurred. The direct costs are those resulting from a particular episode of crime and include the value of any money taken, the value of any property lost or damaged, medical costs for any injuries received, and wages lost due to injury. Note that each of these losses is attributable to a specific incident. The indirect costs of crime involve all changes that are the result of fear or anticipation of future crime. This fear, of course, could be the result of past crime, or more generally the result of the exposure to crime in the community through communication with friends, other victims, the mass media, and so on.

Indirect costs are not as easy to assess as are direct costs. However, it is conceivable that indirect costs are more significant for a victim or institution in the long run. To illustrate, if a library installs a $15,000 security system to prevent anticipated theft, we are dealing with indirect costs. The incident that finally triggered the purchase may have been the loss of less than $100 worth of materials (the direct costs). Although substantial, security costs to individuals and public and private institutions are not the only indirect cost of crime that we pay. According to Conklin:

> Crime also has indirect costs. There is the cost of maintaining the vast but undermanned criminal justice system that processes suspects. There are expenditures for the police, the courts, and the correctional institutions. Aside from these easily measured expenses, there are losses to inmates and to society from time spent in jails and prisons. Inmates working at prison jobs earn only a fraction of the money they could make in the outside world. Not only do they suffer the loss of earning power and dignity, but their families are not provided for and often require welfare assistance, an additional cost to society. Society also suffers in the incarceration of inmates because of the expense of maintaining prisons and their staffs, and because of the loss to the economy of the full productive effort of the inmates.[2]

The cost of maintaining the criminal justice system is overwhelming. Each year, expenditures for criminal justice activities total billions of dollars; over half of this amount is for police protection and services. Not counting the enormous private security force in the country, over one million people are employed in criminal justice related jobs in the public sector. The indirect costs of crime affect all of us. These costs are shared by all taxpayers, not only by victims of crimes and their families.

Certainly these billions of dollars spent on criminal justice have tremendous impact, but they may be felt less on a day-to-day basis than some of the other indirect costs of crime. The changes that people make in their lifestyles because of the fear of crime are disturbing. Again, Conklin describes these in detail:

> The indirect costs of crime also include the changes in attitude and behavior by people who fear their own victimization. They stay off the streets at night and lock their doors. If they go out, they walk only in groups and avoid certain areas of the city. They use taxis or cars to protect themselves from street crime. If they have to drive through high crime-rate areas of the city, they roll up their car windows and lock the doors. To avoid possible victimization, people do not use library and educational facilities at night, they stay away from meetings of social groups and organizations, and they keep out of parks and recreational areas. Some forfeit additional income by refusing overtime work which would force them to go home after dark. Some even carry firearms or knives. Many take security measures to protect their homes—additional locks on doors and bars on windows, brighter lights on porches and in the yards, burglar-alarm systems, and watchdogs. Judging by the types of precautions that people take, they seem to fear personal attack more than the loss of property through theft. One extreme but fairly common reaction to both personal and property crime is a desire to move, to escape from the community where crime poses such a great threat.[3]

Many of these same patterns are evident in public institutions as well as in our homes. The use of security is increasing at a rapid pace. The anxiety felt by employees leads to many work-related problems and impacts on the functioning of the institution.

NATIONAL FINDINGS: DIRECT COSTS

Several items in the national survey asked about information related to the direct costs of crime and disruption in libraries. These included an estimate of the total value of losses due to crime as well as indicators of the effects of crime on services provided. The effects on services were broken down into five categories: closing the library, closing a branch library, changing hours, losing the use of equipment, and stopping existing programs. Respondents were also asked whether police had been called during the past year. Calling police usually has no impact on the budget, but it is an indicator that some situation was perceived as too difficult for the staff to handle alone.

Along with those indicators of the impact or cost of crime, respondents were asked for opinions about how much crime had affected the institution. Data from these items are described below.

Dollar Losses

Respondents were asked to "estimate the total amount lost due to crime and disruption (vandalism, theft, book loss, etc.) over the last 12 months." Response categories ranged from "none" to "over $10,000." Returns showed that the most common response was "less than $100." Twenty-one percent of the sample had some losses, but the losses were under $100. When the latter group was combined with the libraries that reported no losses at all, the size of the group reached one-third of the total. That is, approximately one-third of the libraries reported little or no losses due to crime. At the other extreme, over one-fifth of the sample reported losses over $1,000 (see Table 20). Just under 3 percent reported losses of more than $10,000. The actual impact of the loss is a function of the size of the budget and whether losses are "covered" by using funds allocated for other purposes. As one response indicated: "We had two problems—the building was entered and antiques (ours and a display on loan) were stolen. Total losses of $1,276.00. They're gone forever. Windows and storm windows were broken by stones. A trustee did repair work so our cost was for materials only." Another reported that "The cost must be absorbed in our regular operating budget. If things get vandalized we don't get any extra money to repair them."

Large losses could be the result of either many small-scale episodes or a few costly incidents. One way to clarify these possible patterns is to examine the losses of those libraries known to be in the high-crime categories. If

TABLE 20

PROPORTION OF LIBRARIES REPORTING LOSSES DUE TO CRIME

	Region				
Amount Lost	Northeast	South	North Central	West	Total
$0	14%	10%	11%	11%	12%
Less than $100	20	14	30	22	21
$101–$250	15	19	17	19	17
$251–$500	15	14	15	16	15
$501–$1,000	19	17	9	14	14
$1,001–$2,500	7	13	11	7	10
$2,501–$5,000	6	7	6	5	6
$5,001–$10,000	3	4	1	3	3
Over $10,000	3	4	1	4	3

most of the high-level losses come from this group of libraries, we know that heavy dollar losses are associated with repeated episodes. High-crime libraries were composed of those in the top 10 percent of the scores on the total crime index, those having the most episodes. Over half of the highest dollar losses (over $10,000) were contained in this small group. It appears that high losses tend to be associated with continuous crime rather than with a few costly incidents (see Figure 14). Many of the large losses not associated with continuous incidents were the result of arson.

Were there any regional differences in crime losses? The differences were not major, but once again the north central region appears to have a lower proportion of libraries with major losses. As can be seen in Table 20, only 2 percent of north central libraries reported losses over $5,000; libraries in the other three regions (6–8 percent) were more likely to have losses at least that high. Using $500 as an indicator of significant loss, the survey found that southern libraries were most likely to exceed this amount (45 percent), followed by libraries in the Northeast (38 percent), West (33 percent), and north central area (28 percent). These estimates of dollar losses do not include the cost of implementing or maintaining security systems. Losses are limited to the direct costs of crime—actual losses attributable to specific episodes of known crimes.

Effects of Crime on Services

If crime and the damage caused by crime necessitates altering services normally provided to the public, these changes are considered to be direct

Staggering Security Losses Faced by Metro Toronto

Contending that more money must be budgeted for the staff it needs to protect its holdings, the Metro Toronto Library reports that each year over 12,000 books, films, and musical scores are damaged or stolen. Metro Toronto estimates that the equivalent of 20 percent of its materials budget was lost last year through theft and vandalism. Explains Metro Toronto, library security has become an increasingly difficult problem due to lack of supervisory personnel and the design of the $30 million Metro building, which has three times the space of the old facility and four times the number of users.

Metro Toronto had sought a budget of $13,598,300 to enable it to hire an additional 60 staff members, but it has been granted funding for only ten new permanent employees to replace ten temporaries. But the Metro budget committee has recommended an allocation of only $12.8 million, up 5.7 percent from last year's budget.

The library says that with the $798,300 cut in its budget request it will not be able to buy materials necessary to maintain its collection of more than a million books.

■ Figure 14 From *Library Journal,* June 15, 1981, p. 1269.

---

costs. They are not caused by the fear of future crime, but rather by the direct effects of crimes that have already occurred. Several different indicators of lost services were assessed in the survey. They ranged from a total loss of service for some period of time (closing the library) to minor service impact such as changing hours or losing equipment.

How did administrators assess these effects? The respondents were asked: "In your opinion how much does crime and violence affect your services to the public?" The range of possible responses is shown in Table 21.

TABLE 21

PROPORTION OF LIBRARIES REPORTING VARIOUS EFFECTS OF CRIME

Level of Effect	% of Libraries
Not at all	41.0
Very little	46.4
Moderate	11.0
A great deal	1.6

Vandalism Snuffs Out NLW Plans for Putnam Valley, New York

New York's Putnam Valley Library reports that many of its extensive plans for National Library Week festivities had to be scuttled in the wake of a night of vandalism that left equipment and materials wrecked.

Among the damages: catalog and borrower file cards were strewn throughout the wing of the new building; copy machine ink was smeared on carpeting in three rooms, and a slide projector, carousel, and classical music tapes were destroyed. Also: A fire had been started in a sink, thermostat wires were snipped, and the oil burner dismantled. Working on the outside, vandals tore open a ventilating unit and ripped off a light fixture.

■ Figure 15 From *Library Journal,* June 15, 1981, p. 1269.

Data in Table 21 indicate that nearly 90 percent of responding libraries said that crime and violence affected their services to the public either "not at all" or "very little." Of these two groups, slightly more reported that crime had very little effect. Just over 12 percent of the sample said that crime and violence affected their services to the public "moderately" or "a great deal" (see Figure 15).

What about the experiences of libraries reporting the greatest crime effects? Compared with the overall sample, these facilities have, as expected, more crime and a greater variety of it. For example, although over one-third of the full sample reported no intentional book damage, only 11 percent of the libraries with serious crime effects had no book damage. Likewise, nearly half (46 percent) of the high-effect group had 11 or more episodes of book damage; only 15 percent of the general sample had that many. Patterns of book theft show similar differences. Seventy percent of high-effect institutions had 11 or more episodes of book theft, compared with 38 percent of the total sample. Other types of crime show differences in frequency in the same direction—the higher the reported effect of crime, the more frequent the crime.

Another way to determine if the perceived effect of crime is related to actual crime patterns is to examine the correlation between the amount of crime and the degree of effect on services. A strong relationship would mean that as the amount of crime increased, so did the effect of crime. Correlations were computed for each of the 18 crime items as well as the crime indices. Although each of the separate items did relate to the perception of crime effects, some of the items were more strongly associated than were others.

The librarians responding to the survey were most likely to indicate that the effect of crime was great when intentional book damage was high and reference material was stolen frequently. Several other crime indicators were highly related to the effect of crime, including vandalism inside the building and book theft. The most serious crimes, arson and assault on staff and patrons, were the weakest predictors of the effect of crime. Apparently, even though those are the most feared and serious offenses, they did not affect the functioning of the institution as much as the more frequent but less serious crimes. Similar findings resulted from an examination of the crime indices. The strongest association was between vandalism and the effect of crime; the weakest relationship was between assault and perceived effects. This is consistent with the concerns raised earlier that visible evidence of crime, such as vandalism, has tremendous impact on observers' attitudes about safety and security. In total, all types of crime were related significantly to the perceived effect of crime, but the more visible episodes seem to have the greatest impact on attitudes. In contrast, the impact on the behavior of the staff may be more influenced by crimes that threaten personal safety or personal property. (This possibility is examined later.)

Let us now examine the specific effects of crime. The most serious impact of crime on services provided to the community would be having to close the institution. This extreme response was reported by less than 2 percent of the respondents and the majority of these closed the library only once. We do not know how long the facility was unavailable. Arson was the apparent cause of the closing in many of these cases. There were similar patterns for the closing of a library branch (see Table 22).

Changing the operating hours was more common than closing the library. Here we found that approximately 4 percent changed their schedules due to crime, and several libraries had done this more than once.

TABLE 22

PROPORTION OF LIBRARIES REPORTING EFFECTS OF CRIME

Type of Effect	No. of Times	
	Once	Twice or More
Closed library	1.3%	.3%
Closed branch	1.0	.2
Changed hours	3.1	.3
Lost use of equipment	4.5	3.5
Stopped programs	2.6	2.3
Called police	18.3	26.3
Any of the above	16.6	30.2

When asked whether it ever was necessary to stop a program being run for the public, 5 percent reported that they had done so. About half of these libraries had stopped more than one program.

The final indicator of the direct cost of crime on services was whether the use of equipment had been taken away. Eight percent of those responding indicated that it had, with nearly half reportedly losing the use of equipment more than once. Following are some comments:

> The change in hours prevented any further assaults on librarians. (small New Mexico library)
>
> We're closing earlier at night now. (New Jersey)
>
> Friday evening hours and programs have been severely curtailed at one branch. (Connecticut)
>
> We had to stop our disco dance lessons. (Massachusetts)
>
> A while ago there was a real problem in the library with teenagers. This became a hangout for them and they gave the staff considerable grief. As a result the librarian cut out the night hours and publicized the reasons for her doing so in the paper. When the library reopened several months later, the staff took a strong arm approach—and the problem soon evaporated. (New Hampshire)
>
> Using grant funds, we established a deposit collection at a youth center. The center was closed due to vandalism and lack of staffing. Even if it were opened again, we would not reestablish the collection, because it was ripped off too badly. (city of 50,000)

An index assessing the impact of crime on services was computed by combining each of the items described here. Fifteen percent of the sample had experienced at least one of these problems, and 7 percent more than one.

A somewhat different but still important factor influencing impact of crime was whether the library ever called the police to handle a situation during the year in question. Nearly half (45 percent) had done so at least once. Imagine, almost half of our public libraries have experienced a situation serious enough for them to have called in the police! In 6 percent of the cases, this had happened six times or more during the year.

> The only time we called the police was about a car parked at the library late at night. (New Mexico)
>
> I have called police as soon as a group inside begins acting up. So this has subsided somewhat. (Massachusetts)
>
> The police are called immediately once we determine there are drunks in or around the library. Police are called at least 8–10 times per month. (Texas)

The impact of police presence is mixed. On the one hand, it reassures staff and patrons that they are protected when necessary. But it also indicates that danger may be present and that the library may not be a safe place. Rather than being denied or ignored, these perceptions can be put to positive use by serving as reminders to staff and patrons alike to exercise appropriate caution. The presence of police also may increase the amount of cooperation between the law and the library as police come to recognize the needs of the library for better security.

NATIONAL FINDINGS: INDIRECT COSTS

At the beginning of the chapter, it was suggested that indirect costs, although difficult to measure, can be as devastating to the individual or institution as the direct costs of crime. Indirect costs can be thought of as any change resulting from the anticipation or fear of future crime. This includes changes made in the environment such as security systems or personnel, as well as changes in behavior related to fear. Some of these indirect costs have actual monetary expenses associated with them; others are primarily psychological or personal. A wide range of indirect costs was assessed, including the amount spent on security and crime prevention, the deployment patterns of 14 different security items or programs, and techniques used to avoid victimization by the staff.

Crime Prevention Expenses

The survey asked: "What was the total amount spent on crime prevention in the last 12 months?" including security devices as well as security personnel. Many security systems had been installed more than one year before the survey was received. This estimate then is of an annual expenditure by public libraries for security. A full range of responses was evident (see Table 23). The majority of libraries spent no funds on crime prevention in the 12 months before receiving the survey. At the other extreme, 3 percent spent over $10,000. All told, only 14 percent of the sample spent over $250 that year.

What differentiated libraries with large expenditures from those that spent little? Two patterns emerge. First, libraries that spent over $1,000 on crime prevention tended to be those institutions with chronic crime problems. Second, many of the libraries with high expenditures, as expected, had security personnel, which required a continuing outlay of funds even after security equipment was in place (see Figure 16).

How strong is the relationship between spending for crime prevention and actual reduction or elimination of crime? Unfortunately, the relation-

TABLE 23

TOTAL AMOUNT SPENT ON CRIME PREVENTION IN ONE YEAR

Amount Spent	% of Libraries
$0	74.1
Less than $250	12.1
$251–$500	2.7
$501–$1,000	2.9
$1,001–$2,500	1.5
$2,501–$5,000	2.0
$5,001–$10,000	1.5
Over $10,000	3.0

ship is not that simple. It appears that chronic crime leads administrators to opt for crime prevention programs that tend to reduce the problems; they do not eliminate crime. On the other hand, libraries that were free from crime, according to reports, typically spent nothing on crime prevention. That is, these libraries were free from crime not because they had sophisticated security programs, but rather because they were in low-crime environments. Ninety-eight percent of the libraries reporting no crime also reported that they spent absolutely nothing on crime prevention during the 12 months in question. In contrast, only 34 percent of the high-crime libraries spent nothing on crime prevention. In these cases, expenditures may have been cost-effective had they been made. Thirty percent of the high-crime libraries reportedly spent more than $1,000; 12 percent spent more than $10,000. Note that these libraries spent considerable amounts on crime prevention during the year (and in previous years), but still were in the top 10 percent with respect to overall crime scores. This does not mean, however, that the expenditures were not

The High Cost of Security

An *Associated Press* report tells of the plight of a small library in Maine which decided to sell a valuable Eastman Johnson painting donated in 1953 because it couldn't afford insurance or the kind of security needed to protect it from theft. The Rockport Library, which has an annual budget of $9000, sold the Johnson painting, "Sugaring Off at the Camp," for $320,000. The proceeds of the sale will go into a library trust fund.

■ Figure 16 From *Library Journal,* June 1, 1979, p. 998.

worthwhile. It is likely that in those instances the programs deterred substantial amounts of crime.

Examining the correlation between the amount of crime and the amount spent on crime prevention gives another indication of the relationship between expenditures for crime prevention and the patterns of crime. Once again we find that the greater the expenditure the greater the amount of crime. Each of the 18 different types of crime, on the average, was higher in libraries that spent more to prevent crime. The correlations ranged from .10 for the relationship between assault on staff and crime prevention expenditures, to .38 for verbal abuse of staff. All of these correlations were significant at the .0001 level. That is, a relationship this strong would occur by chance in only 1 in 10,000 times.

It is interesting that the strongest relationship was between verbal abuse and expenditures. Staff that is verbally harassed is most likely to be in libraries that spend large amounts on security. This is also true for other types of crime and disruption, but it is most evident for verbal abuse. It seems to imply that being verbally abused may be more distressing to staff than vandalism or the loss of books and equipment. An alternative interpretation is that libraries with serious crime problems also have serious problems with verbal abuse of staff, which combined leads to security expenditures. In either case, verbal abuse of staff is a good indicator of the likelihood of high expenditures for crime prevention. To illustrate, of those libraries reporting no verbal abuse, less than 2 percent spent over $1,000 on crime prevention. Of those libraries reporting over 10 episodes of verbal abuse of staff, 32 percent spent over $1,000.

Do crime prevention expenditures vary by region? The lowest average expenditures were in the western states. Eighty-five percent reported no expenses for crime prevention and only 4 percent spent over $1,000. Libraries in the north central region were slightly more likely to have crime prevention expenses. Three-quarters spent nothing and 5 percent reportedly exceeded $1,000. A similar proportion of southern libraries spent nothing on crime prevention during the year, but slightly more libraries were spending over $1,000 (7 percent). Libraries in the Northeast were the biggest spenders for crime prevention. Although about two-thirds spent nothing, 15 percent spent more than $1,000. This is twice as high as the next closest region.

Security Patterns

There is a broad range of possible security devices and programs. Fourteen different measures were examined that might have been in operation in each library, from the relatively simple smoke detector and locked storage

TABLE 24

PROPORTION OF LIBRARIES WITH VARIOUS SECURITY MEASURES

Type of Measure	% of Libraries
Closed circuit television	1.3
Plainclothes guards or police	2.9
Portable signaling device	4.1
Uniformed guards or police	4.8
Security screens on all windows	5.3
Unbreakable windows	6.2
Intrusion alarms on all doors	7.8
Book theft detection system	10.0
Automatic communication link with police	11.8
Electronic intrusion system inside	12.6
Security locks on all outside doors	23.0
Police patrol coverage	26.1
Smoke detector	26.6
Locked storage room	37.0

room to the more sophisticated book theft detection systems, intrusion alarms, and closed circuit television.

There are several interesting ways to examine these relevant data. First, we present the patterns of deployment for the various measures, followed by the regional breakdown. Then we describe security patterns in high- and low-crime institutions. The effect of these measures on reducing or preventing crime is highlighted by comparing libraries in comparable cities (controlling for size) that used extensive security with those that used little. In this way, similar libraries with and without security can be compared with regard to their crime scores.

NATIONAL PATTERNS. As expected, the simpler, less expensive security measures were the most widely used. The locked storage room was the most common measure reported (see Table 24). Thirty-seven percent of the sample reported having a room for this purpose. It was not clear, however, that appropriate lock and key controls were implemented. A locked room is most useful when only appropriate and necessary staff have access.

Smoke detectors were in place in only 27 percent of the reporting libraries. Several respondents indicated that although they did not have smoke or fire detection systems, local ordinances that had recently been passed required their installation. The use of some type of police patrol coverage was found in 26 percent of the sample.

These three most common security measures also tend to be the least expensive. Despite the relatively low cost, they can be effective against the types of crime that they are designed to prevent.

The other common type of security measure was the use of security locks on all doors. Just over one-fifth of the responses indicated that all the doors had security locks, and half had security locks on at least some doors. From this point, there is a large decline in the use of the various techniques. Only 13 percent of the sample had an electronic intrusion system. This was about the same proportion that had an automatic communication link with police, which can be very useful during a crisis situation. Following are some comments:

> We can call the custodian and police on a hot line.
>
> In addition to the extra employees in the branch we have a direct line—a direct dial telephone to police and a panic button.
>
> We have a motion intrusion system but it doesn't work until the person is inside.
>
> At one troublesome branch we employ a male watchman.
>
> Police department officers accompany staff on the building lock up routine which takes about ½ hour.
>
> . . . a cooperative police department made a tremendous difference in the situation.
>
> We have no system but we do double check doors and windows to be sure all is secure before leaving.
>
> We added a sentry light . . . [which] cost us $7/month. Plus a small increase in our electric bill for leaving 2 bays of lights on all night.
>
> We have a safe for valuables.
>
> We do have a security system. However, it isn't operable at this time because we have a broken window.
>
> Since the canine patrol was begun two months ago we have had no problems.

Perhaps the best of all was:

> Our library is located in the same building as the police station. So we have around the clock protection.

Earlier it was reported that book theft was one of the most frequent crimes in most libraries. Yet only 10 percent of the sample had operational book theft detection systems. If losses are high enough, these systems can be cost-effective.

The use of security personnel, either uniformed (5 percent) or plainclothes (3 percent) was relatively rare and, of course, quite expensive. Among the least common devices were portable signaling devices and closed circuit television.

A security index was computed to provide information on the overall use of any of the items mentioned in Table 24. The full range of security deployment was found, but most libraries had relatively few devices. In fact, one-quarter of the sample had none of the measures that were asked about—not even a locked room or a smoke detector! An additional 19 percent had only 1 security item and 17 percent had only 2. Nearly three-fourths of the institutions had 3 or less of the security items. At the other extreme, just over 1 percent had 10 or more of the items on programs. Only three libraries had all 14 measures.

Possible changes in the use of security measures were examined by looking at the findings of the two Massachusetts samples (1980 and 1983). Although not all the items were asked in 1980, ten different security items appeared on both surveys. The findings were mixed. There was an increase in the use of the following: portable signaling devices (7 to 13 percent), closed circuit television (0 to 6 percent), security locks on all doors (16 to 28 percent), intrusion alarms on all doors (14 to 25 percent), and security screens on windows (5 to 11 percent). Several security items were less widely used by the 1983 sample, including communication links with police and unbreakable windows. The decrease in library crime in Massachusetts uncovered by the surveys may be due in part to the increased use of these security items.

REGIONAL DIFFERENCES. The security index reveals that north central states were most likely to have no security items in the library (32 percent). This was followed by western states (26 percent), southern states (21 percent), and the Northeast (20 percent). North central libraries also were least likely to have more than five of the designated items. Only 6 percent of the sample reported having at least six different security measures, compared with 9 percent in the South and 10 percent in the West. Libraries in the Northeast indicated that 19 percent had more than five security items.

HIGH-CRIME LIBRARIES. Based on findings noted earlier regarding expenditures for crime prevention, we would expect that libraries with the highest amounts of crime may be those with the most highly developed security systems. Again, the implementation of security programs often is in response to unacceptably high levels of crime. These security programs usually reduce but do not eliminate the problem, or at least reduce some of the problems.

The proportions of high-crime libraries with security measures are shown in Table 25. Note that these proportions tend to be substantially

TABLE 25

PROPORTION OF HIGH- AND LOW-CRIME LIBRARIES WITH VARIOUS SECURITY MEASURES

	% of Libraries	
Type of Measure	High-Crime	Low-Crime
Closed circuit television	2.0	0.0
Plainclothes guards or police	6.6	0.0
Portable signaling device	9.0	0.0
Uniformed guards or police	13.0	1.2
Security screens on all windows	9.2	1.4
Unbreakable windows	1.3	6.6
Intrusion alarms on all doors	19.7	1.3
Book theft detection system	36.0	2.5
Automatic communication link with police	24.4	3.6
Electronic intrusion system inside	25.6	1.2
Security locks on all outside doors	38.5	10.1
Police patrol coverage	34.2	13.6
Smoke detector	59.0	12.7
Locked storage room	67.1	14.5

higher than those in Table 24. In addition, they are dramatically higher than the proportions for the low-crime libraries in Table 25.

As an illustration, the proportion of high-crime libraries that had electronic intrusion systems was 26 percent; the corresponding figure for the low-crime libraries was 2 percent. Similarly, 24 percent of high-crime libraries had automatic communication links with police; only 4 percent of low-crime libraries did so. Even among the less expensive and simpler security items there are striking differences. Fourteen percent of the low-crime, compared with 67 percent of the high-crime institutions had a lockable storage room. Security locks were found in 38 percent of high-crime and 10 percent of low-crime libraries. The relatively low frequency of unbreakable windows is due to the expense of securing every window in the high-crime libraries. Nearly two-thirds of the libraries with low crime had no security devices at all. Only 3 percent of the high-crime libraries had no protection. Why the few high-crime libraries had avoided installing some type of security device is not clear. Perhaps security was intact, but the respondent, because of fear of crime, refused to acknowledge this on the survey. A lack of trust is consistent with repeated victimization. Not knowing how the information might be used, the respondent may have perceived it safer to deny having security measures.

Does the use of security measures reduce or prevent crime, and if so by how much? These are not easy questions to answer. The ideal study would compare crime rates before and after security implementation. In addition, it would include a proper control so that changes, if they did occur, could be attributed to the new security measure and not some other naturally occurring change. That is, from time one to time two, crime may have decreased because of several factors other than or in addition to security, such as a general decrease in crime in the community or an increase in police patrols in the area.

In the absence of such a controlled study, some suggestions can be made from the current data about the effect of security on crime in the library. There are two ways to assess this relationship. First, the respondents were asked: "If you installed security devices or hired security personnel within the last three years, how much has crime and disruption declined?" Second, information about the relationship between having and not having security items and the comparable crime patterns is available from the survey results. As mentioned earlier, it is important to compare similar libraries with and without the items. Ideally, the libraries should be identical except for the use of the item in question.

Approximately 30 percent of the libraries responding had implemented some type of security measure within the last three years. In that group, 75 percent claimed that crime and disruption had not declined at all. The security measures apparently did not reduce crime for the majority of libraries. Two points must be noted. One, we do not know from this item what type of security measure we are assessing. The response could refer to the addition of a smoke detector or an armed guard. Naturally, one would have more impact than the other. Second, during that three-year period in question, crime rates in most locations have risen substantially. The fact that crime did not decrease is not entirely a negative statement about security. Even if the addition of security items prevents the increase in crime that is likely to occur in most libraries, it may have been an effective measure. Twenty percent of the sample that implemented new security measures indicated that crime had been reduced by at least 20 percent; 13 percent indicated that it had been cut in half. One small group is of particular interest. Five percent replied that crime had been cut by 90 percent after security items had been installed.

The second indicator of the effectiveness of security measures shows mixed results as well. Some items do tend to be associated with lower crime rates; others tend to be associated with higher crime rates than in libraries without the item. Correlations between the amount of security and the amount of crime were tabulated for the full sample. Basically, we examined the relationship between the security index and the amount of each type of crime. All of the crime items were related to the amount of security, but as we saw earlier, these relationships were positive. That is, the more security a library had, the more crime it tended to have. The obverse, of course, is true as well—the more crime a library has, the more security it is likely to have. This reinforces the interpretation that security is employed when crime becomes defined as a serious problem.

Staff Victimization

One of the most dramatic effects of crime is the fear and apprehension that may affect the staff and/or patrons of any public institution. Several items in the survey tapped these concerns. Each question measured behavioral changes resulting from the fear of crime as opposed to the attitudes measured previously (estimating impact of crime). Respondents were asked "Do you carry any personal protection device while at work such as a gun, Mace, whistle, etc.?" Five percent indicated that they did carry a protection device. These included guns, whistles, Mace, clubs, flashlights, hornet spray, and others. A slightly higher percentage (7 percent) indicated that they knew someone on the staff who carried a device.

A second indicator was whether the respondent tried to avoid working after dark. Just over 7 percent said that they did, and 12 percent claimed that a staff member had specifically asked not to work after dark. In locations where crime is perceived as a problem, some employees like to be picked up after work as a safety measure. We asked: "Has crime and disruption or the fear of crime caused your being picked up after work for safety reasons?" Less than 10 percent replied that they were picked up. A higher percentage (17 percent) was escorted to their cars after working hours because of their fear of crime. Here are some comments:

> We always keep a second person on the third floor. We limit access to technical and administrative services and staff lounge area by locking elevators and doors during night hours.

> We always have a man close the building.

> I make sure that at least three people are working and they do leave together.

> We don't leave people alone in the building at night and the staff tries to leave en masse.

> We all go together rather than alone.

> The library is never staffed by only one person and after dark the staff does leave together.

> Two staff people work together after dark for protection and have a link-up call with the Sheriff's department.

> We are open two evenings a week from 6–9, and the library is covered by a lone woman. Only once has my assistant been appprehensive about a late patron (male) but no problems occurred. My trustees are aware of a potential problem and a volunteer or teenage help was used for late evenings. Our budget would not allow for an additional paid person at this time for those hours.
>
> We have gone to double staffing so that we'll feel safer during the rush hours.
>
> Some of the staff are picked up because they don't like to leave their cars in the parking lot and no one is to be left in the building or parking areas alone.
>
> We require that our high school pages be picked up at night.
>
> We do many things. 1. Hourly department checks. 2. Eye control of all stairwells. 3. At least two people on a floor at one time. 4. All leave together at the same time, same exit in a group. All leave parking lot at the same time—no one is ever left alone on library grounds or in the building after dark.

Who are the most concerned librarians? There are small but significant differences between males and females in the sample in terms of their reactions to crime. Women were twice as likely to report that they carried a protection device at work. Four percent of the women and 2 percent of the men did so. Women also were more likely to avoid work after dark (5 to 2 percent). In contrast, men reported that they were more likely to be picked up after work due to concerns about safety. Ten percent of the men compared with 7 percent of the women were picked up at work. Note that the combined totals of men avoiding work after dark and being picked up at work are equal to the total of the women avoiding work after dark and being picked up. In both cases, 12 percent of the sample had these reactions to crime. It appears that men were less likely to avoid working after dark but more likely to be picked up since they were working the late hours. The specific protection techniques vary, but men and women are affected almost equally.

Does being victimized in the past affect one's behavior at work? Apparently it does under some conditions. Those librarians who had been the victims of some crime within the facility were more likely to change their behavior than were nonvictimized librarians (see Table 26). Only 2 percent of nonvictims carried a protection device; 3 percent of those victimized once did so, as did 6 percent of those victimized twice, and 17 percent of those victimized three times. Being victimized once apparently did not make one more likely to carry some protection, but being the victim of multiple crimes did.

Attempting to avoid work after dark followed similar patterns. Of those victimized once, 4 percent avoided work. This was the same percentage as for those who had never been victimized. However, multiple victimization

TABLE 26

	PERSONAL RESPONSES TO CRIME IN LIBRARIES			
	% of Respondents			
	Number of Victimizations			
Type of Response	0	1	2	3
Total				
Carry device	2.4	2.9	6.3	16.7
Avoid work after dark	4.6	4.0	10.3	0.0
Picked up after work	6.7	13.1	10.3	25.0
Males				
Carry device	0.0	0.0	20.0	33.3
Avoid work after dark	0.0	3.0	11.0	0.0
Picked up after work	9.0	10.0	11.0	33.3
Females				
Carry device	3.0	4.0	5.0	17.0
Avoid work after dark	5.0	4.0	10.0	0.0
Picked up after work	6.0	13.0	10.0	33.3

again led to an increase in avoiding work after dark (10 percent). Were victims more likely to arrange rides after work for protection? They were. Nonvictims were picked up in 7 percent of the cases compared with 13 percent for those victimized once. The effect was even stronger for those who had been the victims of crime more than once. Ten percent of those victimized twice and 25 percent of those victimized three times were picked up after work.

Findings for the behavioral effects of crime for males and females also can be found in Table 26. In both cases being a victim tends to increase the likelihood of a behavioral response. This is particularly pronounced for males carrying a protective device and for females being picked up after work. These responses are another example of the indirect costs of crime. Even though these responses were heightened by previous victimization, the fear of future encounters with an offender dictates the protective or avoidance behavior.

In summary, the costs of crime are varied. Whenever a crime occurs, there are some costs incurred. How much of an impact direct costs have depends on the relative cost of the episode in relation to the overall expenditures of the institution. The magnitude of indirect costs cannot be assessed easily. The loss of some services may inconvenience many people slightly, but the fear of crime can be tremendously disruptive to an individual or group of employees. Whenever the impact of crime in a public institution is being evaluated, it is essential to assess both the direct and indirect costs since both impact on the institution and those involved with it.

NOTES

1. John Conklin, *The Impact of Crime* (New York: Macmillan, 1975).
2. Ibid., p. 4.
3. Ibid., p. 6.

5 LIBRARY AND COMMUNITY FACTORS AFFECTING CRIME

In Chapter 3 we noted a series of basic crime data findings. Now we will break down these findings to see the actual relationship between the crime patterns and significant variables.

Remember that the most common type of vandalism described in the survey was intentional book damage, with over 25 percent of the responding libraries noting chronic problems. Vandalism outside the building was more common than vandalism inside the building. Book theft was the most common kind of theft as well as the most common problem of any that was measured. More than half of the sample had chronic problems (occurred more than six times per year); over one-quarter of the libraries had more than 20 episodes per year. The theft of reference material was the second most common theft. Problem patron behavior included drug abuse, verbal abuse of staff and patrons, and indecent exposure. Of these, the most common was verbal abuse of staff, followed by verbal abuse of patrons, indecent exposure, and drug problems. Assaults were among the least common crimes uncovered; 8 percent of the sample had one or more known assaults. Arson also occurred infrequently, reported by 4 percent of respondents. Approximately 90 percent of the returned surveys indicated at least one episode of crime and disruption, most with multiple episodes. Inquiries into the patterns of personal victimization of staff while in the library found that just over 20 percent had been the victim of a crime at some time. Males in the sample were more likely than women to have been victimized.

One of the most important questions that criminologists can help to answer is "What conditions or sets of conditions influence patterns of crime?" The survey instrument used for this book allowed us to examine a number of factors that might be related to crime patterns in libraries. These included characteristics of the library itself as well as information about the neighborhood and the community.

STATE-LEVEL DATA

One of the more interesting patterns related to library crime is variation by state. Since all 50 states were included in the study, it is not possible to examine each in detail here. Let us review some of the highlights. (See Appendix B for information about more detailed analyses.)

National crime data prepared by the United States Department of Justice indicate major variations as a function of state identity, and data on library crime are similar in this regard. Some of the most striking differences of all the patterns examined were the differences found between states. However, these data should be viewed cautiously. Even though the sampling procedure was nearly identical for all the states, the samples were collected at different times. Conceivably, some of the resulting differences reflect not only state differences but time trends as well. States were sampled in groups of 10-15, thus providing some comparisons within each time period as well as within the total sample of all 50 states. It is possible, however, that had a state been sampled six months earlier or later, the results would have been different. (This is demonstrated in Chapter 3 by the data from the two Massachusetts samples.)

As an example of the range of state averages, consider the following. The average scores for intentional book damage ranged from .6 in Vermont to 3.2 in Illinois (on the 0-6 scale described in Chapter 3). A score of 3 indicates that the average number of episodes of book damage was 3-5 per library in Illinois. (Actually, the state of Hawaii had even higher scores, but this was based on partial returns. The majority of the Hawaii returns were not available at the time of these analyses. If those returns are similar to the ones now available, Hawaii will have at least one of the highest rates of book damage. This appears to be true of several other crime items as well.) Book theft scores also show wide variation by state. The lowest average score was found in Iowa (1.6) and the highest in California (5.0) (see Table 27).

The theft of reference material was highest in Maryland and lowest in Iowa. Vandalism outside the building was most frequent in Maryland and New Jersey, and least in North Dakota. Illinois had the highest rate of vandalism inside the library, with Iowa the lowest. It should not come as a surprise to learn that Iowa and North Dakota have among the lowest crime

TABLE 27

AVERAGE HIGH/LOW SCORES FOR TYPES OF CRIME AND DISRUPTION

Type of Episode	High State	Score	Low State	Score
Intentional book damage	IL*	3.2	VT	.6
Book theft	CA*	5.0	IA	1.6
Reference material stolen	MD	3.0	IA	.6
Equipment stolen	MD	1.2	NE	.1
Other theft	MD	1.7	VT	.3
Vandalism outside building	MD*	2.2	ND	.7
Vandalism inside building	IL*	2.6	IA	.3
Vandalism of patrons' cars	OH*	.6	5[†]	.0
Vandalism of staff cars	NC	.7	VT	.0
Vandalism of equipment	MA*	.8	TN	.0
Drug use by patrons/staff	CA	1.1	4[†]	.0
Drug sale by patrons/staff	MN	.5	15[†]	.0
Verbal abuse of patrons	CA*	1.6	NE	.1
Verbal abuse of staff	CA/MD	2.2	VT	.3
Indecent exposure	MD	.9	NH	.1
Assault on patrons	CA*	.4	8[†]	.0
Assault on staff	CA*	.2	22[†]	.0
Arson	NY/OH	.2	14[†]	.0

*Preliminary returns from Hawaii show higher scores.
[†]Number of states with identical scores.

rates of all states in the nation, according to the FBI *Uniform Crime Reports*. California and Maryland rates are among the highest.

When considering problems of vandalism against cars of patrons and staff, the highest average scores came from Ohio and North Carolina. Several states had no reports of these episodes. Drug use by staff or patrons was reportedly the highest in California, and the sale of drugs in the library occurred most frequently in Minnesota. Again, a number of states had no reported incidents. Problems of verbal abuse against other patrons were at their peak in California and Florida and lowest in Nebraska. Verbal abuse of staff apparently was most serious in California and Maryland and of least concern in Vermont libraries. New York and Ohio were the prime targets for arson episodes.

There are some interesting state differences when examining the impact of crime. It was not unusual for an entire state sample to be free of certain crime effects. In fact, 30 states never had to close a library as a result of crime and disruption. Twenty of the states reportedly never changed their operating hours because of crime. Among those states that did have these problems, California was most likely to have closed a library, and Tennessee was most likely to have closed a branch due to crime. Changing the schedule occurred most frequently in North Carolina. Losing the use of equipment was most often reported by Massachusetts libraries, and Texas stopped programs for the community more than the other states. When asked about calling in the police, several states were equally high, including Arizona, California, Maryland, Massachusetts, and Texas.

Were there variations in the use of security items? Approximately 40 percent of Rhode Island libraries indicated electronic intrusion alarms; five states had none. This, of course, does not mean that no library in the state of Maine, for instance, has an intrusion alarm; only that none in the sample did. The range of police patrol coverage varied from 10 percent in New Jersey and Oregon to over 40 percent in West Virginia, Maryland, Delaware, Georgia, and Arizona. Book theft detection systems were most widely deployed in Wisconsin, Texas, and California. The highest average expenditures for crime prevention were reported by the samples in Connecticut, New Jersey, Rhode Island, and California.

LIBRARY CHARACTERISTICS

As we know, libraries share certain risk factors with other public institutions. These include ease of public access, holding of valued goods, relative lack of security, and the public library schedule. In addition, certain libraries may be at greater risk than others. The state in which the library is located influences the amount and type of crime and disruption likely to be found there.

Do other measured survey variables also affect crime patterns? To find out, we ran correlations between the crime scores for each of the 18 items (listed in Table 14) as well as the crime indices and all remaining survey items. A positive correlation means that as one variable increased in value, the paired items also increased in value. A negative correlation means that the items tended to change in opposite directions. Correlations imply that there is a relationship between the two variables, but they do not indicate the causal direction of the relationship. If we know that greater spending is associated with less crime, that could mean that either the greater spending results in less crime because of its deterrent effects or that there is less spending on crime prevention when crime is low to start with. The causal link conceivably could be in either of two directions. To determine causation someone could increase the amount spent on crime prevention, maintain control over all other variables, and then measure any resulting change in crime.

Which survey variables showed the strongest relationship with crime patterns? Several stand out, including characteristics of the library and characteristics of the community in which it is located. In this section we examine the findings related to circulation level, number of patrons served, size of staff, and proportion of young, middle-aged, and older patrons using the library. Each of these library characteristics may have some significant relationship to the amount of crime. In addition to amount of crime, it may be that only certain episodes are related to these variables.

Circulation

Each of the 18 different types of crime and disruption shows a strong positive correlation with circulation level. Correlations range from .08 for drug sale to .55 for reference theft. Most are over .30. Theft and vandalism show the strongest relationship.

The strong correlation between the level of circulation and the amount of crime is not surprising. Busy libraries provide more opportunities for illegal activities. Not only are there more victims available to choose from, but the activity level makes it easier to conceal one's actions. Even if the rate of crime remained constant as libraries increased in size, we would still find a higher number of incidents in the larger libraries. When partial correlations controlling for the size of the city were run, this overall strong association between circulation and crime was still apparent for most items. However, the correlations for drug use and drug sale were no longer significant. That is, when comparing libraries from cities of the same size, we found that drug problems were not any more likely to occur in libraries with greater circulation.

Table 28 contains data on the proportion of libraries experiencing three or more episodes of crime as a function of the circulation level. The magnitude of the differences is striking. For example, in libraries with circulation under 5,000, only 16 percent had more than three episodes of book damage. Compare this with the 39 percent having circulation between 26,000 and 50,000. Among those libraries circulating over 98,000 items, nearly 80 percent had at least three episodes of book damage. The range for book theft is as striking—from 32 to 93 percent—and there is a similar pattern for theft of reference material. At each increasing level of circulation, there are more libraries experiencing multiple episodes of reference theft.

Circulation level is an indicator of the activity level within the library, but it may not affect crimes that take place outside the library as much. Crime patterns outside the building, although influenced by what goes on

TABLE 28

PERCENTAGE OF LIBRARIES REPORTING THREE OR MORE DISRUPTIVE EPISODES AS A FUNCTION OF CIRCULATION

Type of Episode	Annual Circulation (in thousands)					
	Under 5	6–10	11–25	26–50	51–98	Over 98
Intentional book damage	16%	27%	23%	39%	50%	78%
Book theft	32	39	47	61	75	93
Reference material stolen	8	10	16	25	45	78
Equipment stolen	4	2	2	2	3	13
Other theft	2	3	8	9	11	26
Vandalism outside building	8	10	15	12	18	40
Vandalism inside building	5	3	7	10	20	45
Vandalism of patrons' cars	0	1	0	2	4	8
Vandalism of staff cars	1	0	1	1	2	9
Vandalism of equipment	2	2	3	2	6	16
Drug use by patrons/staff	4	1	4	4	6	12
Drug sale by patrons/staff	2	1	1	0	2	2
Verbal abuse of patrons	3	2	3	6	11	26
Verbal abuse of staff	5	1	6	14	24	46
Indecent exposure	0	0	0	1	3	15
Assault on patrons	2	0	0	1	1	3
Assault on staff	0	0	0	0	1	1
Arson	0	0	0	0	0	1

inside, may also be affected by actions of people who do not use the library. The rate of vandalism to patron- and staff-owned cars does not increase markedly until the highest circulation levels are reached. To some degree this is true of vandalism outside the building as well. The findings related to vandalism inside the building show a more steady progression as circulation increases. Verbal abuse of the staff and to a lesser degree of patrons shows sizable increases at all circulation levels except the two lowest. Few libraries reported more than three assaults, but the vast majority of those that did had circulations in excess of 98,000. In fact, 23 libraries fell into this category (out of over 1,600), and 16 of them were in the highest circulation category. All of the multiple arson cases were found among high circulation libraries. So circulation is closely tied to the level of crime and disruption. This relationship is strongest for crimes occurring within the library and not quite as strong when crimes occur outside or around the library building.

How does the circulation level of the library relate to the impact of crime on the institution? There were no significant relationships between circulation and closing the library due to crime, closing a branch, changing hours, or stopping programs for the community. These tended to occur in approximately the same proportion regardless of the circulation level. Losing the use of equipment and calling the police were significantly related to the level of circulation. In both cases they were more likely to occur as circulation levels increased.

Level of circulation was a good indicator of the total dollar losses from crime. Although the average losses for libraries circulating less than 5,000 volumes were approximately $100, losses for libraries circulating 98,000 items or more were over $750. Expenditures for crime prevention increased more than 20-fold as circulation increased to the highest levels.

Number of Patrons

Another measure of the activity level of the library is the number of patrons served on a daily basis. We expect to find the same type of relationship between size of clientele and crime rates as found between circulation and crime. The distinction between crimes occurring inside and outside the building is not as crucial here. Several crimes that occur outside, such as vandalism of a patron's car or assault of a patron on library grounds, may be facilitated by having more patrons in the area. As can be seen in Table 29, there is almost a perfect progression in the percentage of libraries reporting crimes and the number of patrons. Reference material was reported stolen by 21 percent of the libraries with less than 20 patrons daily; by 39 percent with 21–30 patrons; 55 percent with 31–50 patrons; 70 percent with 51–100 patrons; 82 percent with 101–250 patrons; and 92 percent with over 250 patrons. The correlations of the crime items with the number of patrons were all highly significant, ranging from .14 to .57. The strongest relationships were for reference theft, book theft, intentional book damage, and verbal abuse of staff, in that order. The increase in theft and mutilation of materials may be due to the increased competition for needed resources that occurs when many patrons vie for the same material. When these disturbing efforts fail to provide the patron with the desired material, verbal abuse of staff might be the next step. This explanation is bolstered by the fact that other theft and equipment theft were not as strongly related to the number of patrons in the library. That is, not all thefts were affected so dramatically by increased patrons, only thefts of resource material. The partial correlation coefficients that controlled for city size were all significant except for drug sales, assault, and arson. This may imply that within cities of the same size, having large numbers of patrons in the area has some deterrent effects for serious crimes. These are the crimes where the perpetrator would not want any witnesses. Busy libraries, although they

TABLE 29

PERCENTAGE OF LIBRARIES REPORTING AT LEAST ONE DISRUPTIVE EPISODE AS A FUNCTION OF NUMBER OF PATRONS

Type of Episode	Number of Patrons Daily					
	Less than 20	21–30	31–50	51–100	101–250	+250
Intentional book damage	40%	48%	60%	74%	83%	91%
Book theft	52	70	77	87	92	96
Reference material stolen	21	39	55	70	82	92
Equipment stolen	7	12	13	22	24	48
Other theft	14	25	25	36	45	56
Vandalism outside building	33	46	48	55	66	77
Vandalism inside building	13	23	34	57	60	75
Vandalism of patrons' cars	1	5	6	13	16	33
Vandalism of staff cars	3	7	11	11	23	41
Vandalism of equipment	5	4	7	15	23	45
Drug use by patrons/staff	2	11	10	13	23	33
Drug sale by patrons/staff	0	2	2	3	6	11
Verbal abuse of patrons	6	12	19	21	44	61
Verbal abuse of staff	14	29	33	46	63	79
Indecent exposure	1	4	7	13	29	51
Assault on patrons	1	3	2	3	10	19
Assault on staff	0	1	2	1	4	12
Arson	0	2	2	3	8	11

offer opportunities for crimes, also are less likely to provide the privacy needed to successfully carry out serious offenses.

The findings on vandalism are interesting. This is where the almost perfect progression breaks down; note that vandalism of equipment actually decreases from the less than 20 to the 21–30 category. Other vandalism shows small decreases as the number of patrons increases from less than 10 to less than 20. Data for less than 10 patrons are not shown in Table 29, but in each case the vandalism crime scores were lowest for less than 20 patrons. It appears that the nearly empty library is more likely to be vandalized than the library that has a few patrons each hour. The presence of others, up to a point, does act as a deterrent to crime. Beyond 50 patrons per day, the rates of vandalism increase more rapidly. Considering libraries in cities of all sizes, we find that the rate of assault against patrons or staff also remains relatively constant until there are over 100 patrons a day using the facility.

Does the number of patrons using the library each day increase the impact of crime? In some cases, yes. Correlations significant at the .001

level were found for the relationship between the number of patrons and losing the use of equipment, stopping programs for the community, and calling the police. There also was a significant but not as strong relationship between number of patrons and having to close the library. A strong correlation between total dollar losses and number of patrons was noted (.59), as well as for the amount of money spent on crime prevention (.38). In both cases, as the number of patrons increased, the dollars lost and spent increased.

Staff Size

The third indicator of the activity level of the library is the size of the staff. The survey asked about the number of professional librarians, aides, security people, and other staff. Is there a relationship between problems in the library and staff size? First, let us look at the size of the professional staff. It is clear that as the number of librarians increases, the magnitude of the crime and disruption also tends to increase. This is another good example of the importance of interpreting correlations correctly. This does not suggest that increased staff causes an increase in crime problems. Rather, the conditions, such as size of the library, city size, circulation level, and so on, which lead to having a large staff, also lead to higher crime. The size of the staff is a good indicator of the probable crime level and suggests that larger staff size as opposed to smaller staff size is a risk factor.

Correlations between the number of librarians and various types of crime all were significant at the .001 level. The correlations ranged from .10 for drug sale to .48 for reference theft. The number of professional librarians on the staff also was related to the impact of crime, but not to all of the impact items. A larger professional staff was associated with a greater likelihood of closing a branch, losing the use of equipment, stopping programs, and calling the police. It was not related to having to close the library and changing the operating hours. Strong correlations were found between the number of librarians and total dollar losses due to crime (.47) and crime prevention expenditures (.43).

In addition to the correlations, the proportions of libraries with different size staffs that had episodes of crime were examined. That is, we ran cross-tabulations between staff size and amount of crime. The pattern is clear. At each higher level of number of librarians, the proportion of libraries experiencing each of the various types of crime is greater. For example, in libraries with no professionals, 55 percent reported at least one act of book theft. This increased to 70 percent among libraries with 1 professional, 80 percent if there were 2 librarians, and 93 percent if there were 3–5 librarians. In those libraries with more than 20 librarians, 98 percent had book theft. This general pattern was typical of each type of crime.

TABLE 30

PROPORTION OF LIBRARIES REPORTING AT LEAST ONE EPISODE OF CRIME AS A FUNCTION OF STAFF SIZE

Type of Episode	No. of Librarians				No. of Security Personnel			
	0	1	2	3–5	0	1	2	3–5
Intentional book damage	28%	57%	65%	80%	65%	90%	92%	92%
Book theft	55	70	80	93	79	90	100	75
Reference material stolen	29	46	61	83	61	87	92	82
Equipment stolen	17	14	18	25	20	48	42	33
Other theft	15	23	33	48	31	70	25	83
Vandalism outside building	15	46	53	62	53	73	82	67
Vandalism inside building	13	29	46	61	46	77	73	67
Vandalism of patrons' cars	0	6	14	17	11	48	25	25
Vandalism of staff cars	14	7	13	21	14	44	33	25
Vandalism of equipment	6	8	13	25	14	44	45	54
Drug use by patrons/staff	14	10	13	21	13	40	58	18
Drug sale by patrons/staff	4	2	3	5	3	15	9	27
Verbal abuse of patrons	14	14	25	35	25	74	67	67
Verbal abuse of staff	14	29	44	59	43	83	93	67
Indecent exposure	0	6	12	25	16	49	50	45
Assault on patrons	0	2	5	9	6	35	42	33
Assault on staff	0	2	2	3	2	16	17	17
Arson	0	2	4	5	3	12	11	0

Table 30 shows the proportions of libraries reporting crimes for several levels of staff size up to 3–5 librarians. At higher levels of staffing, not shown in Table 30, crimes continue to appear more frequently. Vandalism inside was reported by 61 percent of libraries with 3–5 librarians and 80 percent of libraries having over 20 professionals. Verbal abuse of the staff jumped from 59 percent with 3–5 librarians to 89 percent if there were more than 20. Indecent exposure was reported by 25 percent and 74 percent of libraries in these same categories. Even assaults on staff increased, from 3 percent in libraries with 3–5 professional staff to 25 percent when more than 20 librarians were employed.

The size of the security staff also was related to patterns of crime and disruption. However, this relationship was not as simple as that for the number of librarians. The correlation between security staff size and each of the crime items was significant. However, these correlations generally were not as high as those found for the number of librarians and crime. The exceptions were the correlations between the number of security personnel and the most serious crimes, assault on patron and staff and arson, which were higher.

In Chapter 4 we examined the relationship between security programs and the amount of crime in the library. Basically, those libraries with the higher amounts of crime also tended to be the libraries with the most security. So security programs apparently are implemented as the need arises. The positive relationship between the number of security personnel and the amount of crime reinforces this view. Again, this suggests that unacceptably high levels of crime lead to the hiring of security people. It may be that a very strong need has to be demonstrated before funds will be allocated for security personnel. In some cases it takes a local crisis to muster enough support for hiring. Only after assaults took place did several libraries indicate that "now" they would be able to hire security people on a full-time or part-time basis. This is consistent with the statistical findings. The strongest correlation with assaults on patrons and staff was with the number of security people in the library. It appears that threat to personal safety is the key to deploying security forces within the facility.

Aside from the correlations, other interesting patterns were related to the use of security personnel. Crime continued to increase with each increase in the number of librarians, but this was not always the case with security people. As seen in Table 30, there was a general increase in crime from those libraries with no security personnel to those having up to two security officers. Beyond that level, crime tends to stabilize and in some cases even declines. Intentional book damage is a case in point. Of the libraries with no security personnel, 65 percent reported book damage. This increased to 90 percent with 1 guard and 92 percent with 2–5 security personnel. Only 70 percent of those libraries with more than 10 security people reported book damage. Similarly, book theft tends to drop in libraries with more than 2 security people. This can be seen for equipment theft, reference theft, and to some degree other theft. Most types of vandalism, assault, and arson also demonstrate this pattern. Although assaults against the staff tend to level off once a second security person is added, they do occur less frequently in libraries with more than 5 guards. This does not mean that rushing to add a second or third security person will guarantee lower crime. A careful review of the type and frequency of the problem must first be made. If there are no unusual circumstances, then additional security people, if adding them is feasible, may provide the deterrent that is missing with only one or no personnel.

Age of Patrons

As shown in the crime patterns noted in Chapter 1, the young are disproportionately involved in crime. They are more likely to be the perpetrators as well as the victims of crimes. Does having a high percentage of youth in the building influence the problems found in that library? Comments from many librarians seem to indicate that it does. One of the survey items asked for an estimate of the proportion of patrons under the age of 18. If this is a high-risk group, then crime should be higher in those libraries with more youth using the facility.

The findings are somewhat surprising. Correlations between the proportion of patrons under age 18 and crime scores indicate that as the number of young patrons increases, the crime level decreases. This is inconsistent with both the national crime statistics and the comments of the survey respondents. Why? The answer seems to be in the survey question itself. It asked about the proportion of patrons under the age of 18, which, of course, includes 17-year-olds as well as infants, 3-year-olds, and many others. And many of these patrons are below that high-risk age group. If the survey had asked about the proportion of patrons between 14 and 18, we would have had a better estimate of a high-risk age group. It does appear, however, that having a large number of children among patrons tends to result in lower crime scores.

Another interesting result is related to patron age. As the proportion of patrons between the age of 19 and 55 increases, several measured crimes also tend to increase. That is, as a library has fewer children and fewer elderly, some crimes increase. Specifically, crimes of theft tend to occur more when the proportion of 19–55-year-olds is high. Correlations between the proportion of these patrons in the library and book theft, reference theft, and other theft are all significant. There also are positive correlations between the amount of drug use in the library, abuse of staff, indecent exposure, and the proportion of 19–55-year-olds. The proportion of patrons between 19 and 55 also is related to the level of crime expenditures. The larger this group, the more the library tends to spend on crime prevention, and the greater the total dollar losses as well.

Examining the proportion of older patrons and crime patterns shows the expected negative relationship. For every crime item except assault against a patron, the higher the proportion of patrons over 55, the lower the rate of crime. A large proportion of older patrons, however, tends to be related to more assaults against a patron.

Many library characteristics were shown to be related to crime patterns. Generally, the busier and larger the library, the more problems with crime and disruption. It is important to keep in mind that we are discussing absolute levels of crime. If a large library has 10 episodes of "other theft," that may, in reality, be a lower theft rate than for a smaller library with 5 episodes. Losing 100 out of 2,000 books, compared with losing 1,000 out of 1,000,000, not only is a higher rate but may actually have a more serious impact on the budget or services of the institution. So these problems must be viewed in the proper perspective. What is a tolerable level of crime (if any level, indeed, is tolerable) varies. One California library in the survey reported losing over 5,000 volumes, having more than 10,000 items damaged, hundreds of episodes of reference theft, as well as chronic vandalism. But this respondent could not answer the question "When do most problems with crime occur?" because "We don't really have problems here!"

COMMUNITY CHARACTERISTICS

Just as certain characteristics of the library are related to patterns of crime, neighborhood and community characteristics may also increase the risk of crime in the library. However, unlike library characteristics, such variables as city size, location of schools and police stations, and neighborhood social class are not under the library's control. Rather, they are among the factors that determine the necessity of preventive action to deter higher incidences of crime and disruption.

City Size

Other things being equal, there are higher crime rates in American cities than in smaller towns, with the difference most pronounced for crimes of violence. Does this pattern hold when examining crimes in libraries as a function of city size?

First, let us examine the correlations between city size and the various crimes. Without doubt, there are strong relationships here. Each of the items and the indices show significant relationships. The correlations range from .15 for assault against a staff member to .54 for the theft of reference material. The correlations with the indices are equally as strong. Each of the correlations between city size and the theft, vandalism, problem patron, verbal abuse, and total indices is above .50. There also are strong relationships between the size of the city in which the library is located and the amounts lost due to crime and spent on crime prevention. Finally, each of the separate measures of the impact of crime was related significantly to city size. The strongest relationships were with having to call the police, losing the use of equipment, and stopping programs, in that order.

Patterns of crime related to city size were examined, first, by average crime scores for each of the separate items and several of the indices, and then by proportion of libraries reporting three or more episodes. This second measure provides information about the possibility that city size is related to number of multiple crimes within the institution. Average crime scores reported in Table 31 are based on the seven-point scale used in the survey (0=never; 6=over 20 episodes). Two types of patterns appear in this table. Theft of equipment, book damage, other theft, outside vandalism, vandalism to staff-owned cars, drug sales, indecent exposure, both kinds of assault, and arson all show no dips in the average scores. Several remain constant at one or more levels of city size, but there are no de-

TABLE 31

AVERAGE CRIME SCORES AS A FUNCTION OF CITY SIZE*

Type of Episode	Under 2.5M	2.5–10M	10–50M	50–100M	100–500M	Over 500M
Intentional book damage	1.0	1.8	3.3	3.5	3.5	3.8
Book theft	1.9	3.1	4.5	5.0	4.6	4.3
Reference material stolen	.1	1.5	3.0	3.6	3.4	3.7
Equipment stolen	.1	.3	.6	.8	1.0	1.3
Other theft	.3	.6	1.1	1.1	1.5	2.1
Vandalism outside building	.7	1.0	1.8	2.1	2.1	2.5
Vandalism inside building	.3	.8	2.0	2.3	1.8	2.1
Vandalism of patrons' cars	.0	.1	.1	.7	.6	.8
Vandalism of staff cars	.1	.1	.5	.6	.7	1.0
Vandalism of equipment	.1	.2	.7	1.0	.8	.8
Drug use by patrons/staff	.1	.3	.5	1.0	1.2	.6
Drug sale by patrons/staff	.0	.0	.1	.3	.3	.3
Verbal abuse of patrons	.1	.3	1.0	1.5	2.0	1.9
Verbal abuse of staff	.3	.8	2.0	2.3	2.7	2.5
Indecent exposure	.1	.2	.5	1.0	1.1	1.2
Assault on patrons	.0	.0	.1	.2	.4	.4
Assault on staff	.0	.0	.1	.1	.2	.2
Arson	.0	.0	.1	.1	.1	.3
Summary						
Theft	2.8	5.3	8.9	10.3	10.5	11.5
Vandalism	2.0	4.0	8.5	9.6	9.7	10.7
Problem patron	.5	1.5	3.7	5.9	6.7	5.8

*Based on 7-point scale: 0 = never, 6 = more than 20 episodes.

creases in the average scores. Notice that this list includes all of the most serious crimes that the survey measured. The same pattern holds for the theft and vandalism indices.

The second pattern is one in which the crimes tend to peak at either the 50,000–100,000 or 100,000–500,000 population level. Then there is a moderate decrease in the average score for the larger cities. This is true for book theft, vandalism inside the building, vandalism of equipment, reference theft, and drug use.

The proportion of libraries in different size cities that reported multiple episodes shows similar patterns. First, some crimes tend to increase as city size increases. This is true for equipment theft, outside vandalism, assault, and arson. All of the most violent crimes fall into this category, including the crimes that are most difficult for the library to control. With the exception of equipment theft, they occur outside as well as inside the building. Overall, the effect of city size on crime is substantial. Not only are the correlations high, but the breakdown of crime scores and the proportion of libraries having repeated episodes show the impact.

Location of Schools

Since libraries share many of the same problems that plague other public institutions, it may be that these problems spill over from one setting to another. If schools have problems with crime, perhaps libraries in proximity to schools also have these problems. Being close to a school also means that there are more youth in the area before and after school hours than if the school were located farther from the library. This may contribute to higher levels of certain types of crime, namely, those likely to be committed by young people.

Since we already know that crime is affected by city size, the comparisons of the effect of being close to a school will be done for cities of the same size. Data in Table 32 compare the crime problems in libraries close to and farther away from a junior high school. In small towns (under 2,500) several of the items are more prominent when the library is in the same block as the school, including book damage, reference theft, vandalism outside and inside, and verbal abuse of the staff. In larger cities, only book damage seems to be affected by proximity to a junior high school. It may be that in larger cities, where crime rates are already high, having a school nearby adds little to the problems of the area. Why some of the problems occur more frequently when schools are farther away is not clear.

The influence of high school proximity is different than that of the junior high school (see Table 33). In small towns, book damage and reference theft are higher when the high school is close by. In the larger cities, book theft and vandalism inside the building are highest when the high school is on the same block and lowest when it is over a half mile away. Although these findings are not as striking as those for city size, it may be important to consider location of schools when planning for the security of the library, especially with regard to the protection of books and reference materials.

Location of Police

Does proximity to the police reduce or deter library crime? There are some indications that this is the case. Again, libraries in similar size cities are compared. In towns with less than 2,500 people, book theft occurred in 47 percent of the libraries within sight of the police station and 90 percent of those more than half a mile away. Similar patterns hold for reference theft (32 percent *vs.* 64 percent), vandalism outside the building (37 percent *vs.*

TABLE 32

PERCENTAGE OF LIBRARIES REPORTING AT LEAST ONE EPISODE OF DISRUPTION AS A FUNCTION OF CITY SIZE AND PROXIMITY TO JUNIOR HIGH SCHOOL

City Size and Type of Crime	Location of School		
	Same Block	Within Sight	Over ½ Mile Away
Under 2,500			
Book damage	48	43	37
Book theft	48	67	62
Reference theft	43	25	30
Vandalism outside	48	38	41
Vandalism inside	29	17	18
Verbal abuse of staff	23	13	19
10,000–50,000			
Book damage	100	93	83
Book theft	94	96	93
Reference theft	82	89	85
Vandalism outside	59	73	68
Vandalism inside	59	71	67
Verbal abuse of staff	59	61	71

TABLE 33

PERCENTAGE OF LIBRARIES REPORTING AT LEAST ONE EPISODE OF DISRUPTION AS A FUNCTION OF CITY SIZE AND PROXIMITY TO NEAREST HIGH SCHOOL

City Size and Type of Crime	Location of School		
	Same Block	Within Sight	Over ½ Mile Away
Under 2,500			
Book damage	58	41	41
Book theft	63	67	67
Reference theft	53	29	25
Vandalism outside	37	27	51
Vandalism inside	26	12	30
Verbal abuse of staff	26	15	32
10,000–50,000			
Book damage	91	95	85
Book theft	100	95	92
Reference theft	91	82	86
Vandalism outside	70	82	64
Vandalism inside	78	74	68
Verbal abuse of staff	64	77	66

58 percent), and verbal abuse of staff (19 percent *vs.* 33 percent). In cities of 10,000–50,000 people, these differences do not appear. For example, book theft was reported by 95 percent of the libraries within sight of the police station and by 92 percent of those farther away. Only vandalism outside the building was substantially greater for libraries farther away from police.

Neighborhood Social Class

Respondents were asked to describe the socioeconomic class of the neighborhood in which the library was located. With just a few exceptions, the relationship between social class and crime problems in the library is negative. That is, as social class tends to go up, crime problems tend to go down. The strongest relationship is with vandalism, followed by verbal abuse and problem patron behavior. There is also a negative correlation between the amount of losses and socioeconomic class. This is true of expenditures for crime prevention as well, which are highest in lower-class areas.

The proportions of libraries reporting at least one disruptive episode are shown in Table 34. Although proportions tend to decrease as social class

TABLE 34

PERCENTAGE OF LIBRARIES REPORTING AT LEAST ONE DISRUPTIVE EPISODE AS A FUNCTION OF NEIGHBORHOOD SOCIAL CLASS

	Type of Neighborhood (Class)				
Type of Episode	Lower	Lower-Middle	Middle	Upper-Middle	Upper
Intentional book damage	91	69	64	70	40
Book theft	81	83	80	81	43
Reference material stolen	85	66	59	66	33
Equipment stolen	24	27	17	22	14
Other theft	50	41	29	33	10
Vandalism outside building	78	59	50	56	33
Vandalism inside building	68	46	39	51	24
Vandalism of patrons' cars	24	18	9	13	9
Vandalism of staff cars	33	22	12	14	5
Vandalism of equipment	33	21	13	19	9
Drug use by patrons/staff	29	21	11	18	0
Drug sale by patrons/staff	12	6	2	3	5
Verbal abuse of patrons	47	33	24	24	19
Verbal abuse of staff	41	51	41	47	33
Indecent exposure	26	20	14	18	19
Assault on patrons	6	10	4	4	0
Assault on staff	4	3	2	2	0
Arson	9	6	3	5	0

increases, one major exception is the proportion of libraries in upper-middle-class areas reporting problems. These libraries are at least as high as those in middle-class areas for all of the items and higher for 15 types of crime and disruption. Other notable items include book theft patterns and verbal abuse of staff. Book theft decreases only in upper-stratum neighborhoods, which comprised only 20 libraries in the sample. So few cases should be viewed cautiously since percentages can fluctuate markedly due to only one or two respondents. Verbal abuse of staff tends to be higher as the socioeconomic class of the area increases.

Data from the national survey show that many of the characteristics of the library as well as of the surrounding community can impact on crime and disruption patterns. Libraries, like other public facilities, do not exist in isolation. What happens in the community can affect the public institution. As discussed in Chapter 6, it would be wise for those concerned with crime and disruption to be aware of the kinds and severity of problems in the area around the library.

6 PROTECTING THE LIBRARY

This chapter reviews several of the major studies on security in libraries. These studies vary widely in terms of complexity. Some focus on a single library; others involve surveys of several libraries or library systems. Our concerns here are mostly with those studies that examine techniques other than book theft detection and physical alarms. Several good reviews of these materials are available in other sources.[1]

First, let us review our survey results on the most serious problems faced by some of the nation's libraries and the solutions adopted by them. Then we will look at general crime prevention programs and some low-cost prevention systems that might be helpful for libraries.

CURRENT FINDINGS

What major findings stood out from the Library Crime Research Project on public libraries? Several important points should be noted. First, a variety of security devices and programs are used in libraries today to help prevent crime. Generally, the more expensive the program, the less likely it is that the library will have it—so money is a factor. For example, the most common security item is a locked storage room, followed closely by smoke detectors and police patrol coverage. Each of these measures is relatively low cost. Only 11 percent of the survey respondents indicated use of electronic intrusion alarms. Even fewer institutions used security personnel. Nearly 25 percent had none of the security items noted in the survey.

Second, libraries that experience more crime not surprisingly tend to have more security. The greatest variety of security programs is in those libraries that fall into the high-crime category. In contrast, crime-free libraries tend not to have any security program. Expenditures for security often were less than the annual losses from crime and disruption. That is, when asked to estimate the total losses from all acts of crime and disruption, many libraries noted losses far in excess of expenditures for security programs.

Third, patterns of security do not always match patterns of crime. A library may have the most problems with book theft, but that does not necessarily mean that any book theft protection is being used, either automatic or manual.

Other Surveys

Several years before this survey, an extensive study of users of electronic theft detection systems was carried out by Louis Romeo. A major goal was to "learn of the practical experience of library users of these systems." This was not an attempt to assess the use patterns of varied security measures, but rather to examine the experiences of known users.

Most of the sample was identified through the manufacturers of various electronic theft detection systems, including some additional institutions known to have the appropriate systems. Questionnaires were sent to 215 libraries and 135 responded. A strength of the survey lies in its sample of a varied group of libraries in universities, small colleges, medical and law facilities, and public and school libraries. Detailed information on the various manufacturers, their systems, costs, and technical data is included in Romeo's series of articles published in Library and Archival Security.[2]

Although there were differences in the effectiveness and problems generated by the systems in the different types of libraries, many of the conclusions reached by the users were similar. The cost of book theft protection typically was estimated to be less than the losses would have been without the system. In some cases the cost was effectively neutralized within a one-year period; in other cases a longer payback time was suggested. The relative speed of the payback was in part determined by the annual loss rate, which varied from about 2 percent to nearly 30 percent! But the trend was clear. Cost-effectiveness was of major importance for most of the libraries. Also, the initial cost of the system was mentioned by many respondents as a major factor influencing their selection of one system over another. Simplicity of operation and perceived reliability also were important issues.

Many of the problems with the systems were shared by the various libraries. Attempts to compromise the systems were of concern in most institutions. Librarians with students as clientele claimed that it was not unusual for them to try to "beat the system." Many techniques used by students and others can be neutralized by an alert and properly trained staff. The addition of book theft detection facilitates the job of the staff with regard to security, but it does not eliminate it. The specific techniques used to compromise the system depended in part on the particular system in use. Yet several of these appear to be rather common responses:

Holding books above and below detector fields.

Passing materials around the system.

Throwing materials out windows for retrieval.

Bypassing secure exits.

Using an accomplice on staff.

Mutilating the sensitizing device.

Removing sensitized covers.

Most of these tactics can be effectively countered by an alert staff member willing to confront the suspected patron. Willingness to confront a patron is a crucial issue. Many book thieves attempting to circumvent security take advantage of the fact that their belligerence will likely discourage intervention. According to Romeo:

> Librarians state that the electronic theft detection system works most effectively when all circulation personnel are totally committed to the concept of library collection security. Training of staff in the operation of the system must be thorough. The stickiest problem for the staff, of course, is their interaction with library patrons when the alarm sounds. A diplomatic statement about the patron's neglecting to check out books should be made without any implication of the possibility of theft.[3]

False alarms also were a problem in many libraries. It was not unusual to have as many as 35–50 false alarms per month in a busy library. Typical triggers included failure to properly charge out books, books from other libraries triggering the response, and activation by briefcases, calculators, and other items. Many respondents felt that false alarms were tolerable given the overall effectiveness of their systems in reducing theft.

Another problem concerned the fact that electronic theft detection may increase the motivation to mutilate materials. Given what we know about the personal needs and orientations of those who do mutilate, it is likely that these same persons will find theft prevention to be an added frustration. One way of dealing with it is to remove some of the needed material as opposed to stealing the book. Romeo found instances in which mutilation appeared to increase, as well as cases in which the addition of theft prevention systems did not facilitate mutilation. When such a system is deployed, the demand for inexpensive photocopying facilities will increase. Meeting this new demand may forestall additional mutilation.

Articles in the *American Library Association Yearbook* show that book theft detection systems are in use in thousands of libraries. According to Knight: "Colleges, universities, and large public libraries were initially the major purchasers of security systems. With the availability of lower priced systems, there has been an increase in the high percentage of sales to junior colleges, high schools, and even junior high and elementary school libraries."[4] Knight's later reports indicate continuing high interest in the use of security systems, and sales continue to increase.[5]

DEALING WITH MAJOR PROBLEMS

A great deal of attention has been given to the patterns of crime and their correlates. What do administrators claim are the most serious problems facing their libraries? How have they tried to combat these problems?

What is considered a serious problem from an administrative standpoint may not be the most common concern among libraries. A serious problem also may not be the most serious offense in terms of legal codes. Rather, the major problem is likely to be the one that has the greatest impact on the normal day-to-day functioning of the library. Describing the frequency of many offenses gave an overall picture of crime and disruption in libraries. To assess the most serious problems, an additional survey was taken of 30 of the nation's major libraries. In May 1983, a brief questionnaire was mailed to the directors of these facilities. Only two questions were asked:

1. Would you describe what you consider to be your most serious problem with crime and/or disruption?
2. How have you attempted to control this problem?

Respondents were advised to withhold identity if desired. In addition, for those who had no objection, a check-off method was used to obtain permission to quote and/or identify the library in question.

Two types of problems overwhelmingly were singled out as the most serious. Problem patron behavior and theft of various kinds were mentioned by 60 and 35 percent of the libraries respectively. Of those libraries not indicating either of these as the most serious problem, one mentioned arson and one indicated that vandalism was the crucial issue. A variety of techniques for controlling these problems was described and should prove useful to other libraries.

First, let us look at the problems of and attempted solutions to disruptive or disturbing patrons. The behavior associated with problem patrons ranged from loitering to drinking to bathing in the rest rooms and sexual activity. One major Massachusetts library described its problems in this way:

> Disruption by two classes of users provides the most easily observable (though not necessarily measurable) daily disturbance to the public. The first class is youngsters aged roughly 11–15, who stop at the library after school (beginning around noon), are boisterous, and frequently cannot be controlled (due to too many exits and not enough staff). We also have many "legitimate" homework doers who are not in this category. We believe that many youngsters are here because there is no one at home, they have no after school employment or activities, and the library provides a free (and warm) environment for hanging around. Not only do they do real vandalism to the public restrooms and the stacks, but they are an annoyance and source of anxiety to older (particularly elderly) users. The other disruptive class is quieter, but even less attractive: male vagrants who arrive at opening time and are ushered out the door when we close. We have continuing problems with this group, the worst of which is the effect they have on the library's ambience. We suspect that they make other users (particularly teenaged girls and elderly women) uncomfortable, and we wonder how many users do not come in at all because of the unpleasant atmosphere in some sections of the library.

What has been done to try to curb these problems? Note that some of these "solutions" are low cost, having little impact on the budget of the institution. Other programs are more costly.

> We try to be tough with the kids. We throw them out, when we can catch them. What we need is a full time youth worker who would organize the youngsters for productive volunteer work in the library. Done in the right style of sympathetic forcefulness, this might work. We have tried to shepherd the older vagrants into one section of the library by putting the newspapers which they read there. The section was chosen because staff people work nearby, and because it is a "pass through" area which is not a discreet room unto itself. The staff thinks this is the best yet of several attempted solutions tried over the years.

"Being tough" with kids who are disruptive certainly can be effective. It should be pointed out, however, that what some kids consider tough and what some public administrators consider tough are at opposite ends. Some of the most disruptive youth are likely to perceive that being thrown out when they are caught is anything but tough—they do not respond to such sanctions. On the other hand, the more moderate youthful offender may respond quite well to having his or her use of the library taken away, even for a short time. Identifying those children who continue to abuse library rules, even after being thrown out repeatedly, would facilitate taking stronger action when necessary.

A major library in the Southeast described its difficulties with problem patrons in this way: "As with most urban library systems, Atlanta Public Library has had its share of loiterers, indigents, and others who harass and intimidate both staff and patrons. Incidents have run the gamut from physical assaults to exposures and use of the restrooms for bathing and other activities." Control of this problem focused on a cooperative effort with Atlanta police.

> The Atlanta Public Library has taken aggressive measures to eliminate these problems. We have had regular and productive meetings with members of the Atlanta Police Department, including the Chief of Police. The APD has assigned one officer full time to the Central Library, and other officers "drop in" on a regular basis to our branches. In addition we have a private security service which assists in monitoring Central Library and have recently appointed a security coordinator on the library staff. Our primary goal is to prevent incidents and the visibility of police officers has assisted us to do that. When incidents occur we do prosecute offenders. This too has resulted in improvements in the situation.

Several important steps were taken by the Atlanta Public Library. Regardless of the size of the system, cooperation with local police can be very effective. Unfortunately, police departments may not always perceive that the library's problems are as serious as in other institutions or private settings. A careful description of the problems and their effect on citizens, many of whom may be influential within the community, may be necessary. Once a cooperative program is established, the presence of police in the library both deters offenders and reassures staff. At times a random drop-in may be preferable to the "drop in on a regular basis" of the Atlanta plan. Prosecution of offenders who commit acts that the library views as serious also can be effective. Effectiveness increases when these prosecutions are both successful and visible to other potential offenders. Adequate publicizing of prosecution and resulting penalties is fruitful.

A similar program was developed by the Central Arkansas Library System. Its most serious problem involved disruptive behavior. One response was to increase contact with local police.

> Our most serious problem occurs in the downtown library. . . . [It involves behaviors that] range from stolen car batteries, to indecent exposure, to a physical attack on the security guard which resulted in his having a concus-

sion. Contributing factors include the proximity of a commercial plasma bank and a free lunch program at a nearby church-sponsored mission. Declining funding for human services programs including mental health facilities, correctional institutions, substance abuse programs, etc., coupled with high unemployment have put an ever increasing number on the streets who have more serious behavior problems than we observed even three years ago. I would characterize our most serious problem as disruptive behavior from persons having mental health problems and/or criminal records ranging from merely annoying to violent and potentially violent. We are seeing an increase in the potentially violent.

Full administrative support [is given to the] security guard and other staff members to increase their ability to use their judgment and react quickly without fear of "doing the wrong thing." We have met with and established an excellent rapport with the local police department so that they respond immediately to calls for assistance. The police also patrol the downtown building and grounds on a random basis so that our problem population cannot anticipate when they will appear. We have also filed formal complaints where indicated and will not hesitate to do so in the future. Of two complaints filed last year, one resulted in a restraining order prohibiting the individual from entering any public building. The other resulted in a one year jail sentence plus a hefty fine for the individual. The "street grapevine" seems to distribute this information, as things have calmed down for extended periods of time after such action. We also do not hesitate to ask disruptive persons to leave immediately and call police if they do not comply. We are in the process of planning a full day training session for all system staff in the fall.

Police presence and prosecution may not be necessary if problems with offensive patrons are less severe. A different tactic was adopted by the Tampa Public Library in Florida.

Those library users variously described as "casual readers," "problem patrons," or "bums" by their appearance and aroma frequently upset other patrons. While incidents of "flashing" or assault occur once in a great while, the most constant complaint is the mere presence of vagrants and winos. [To control the problem] we have moved a substantial portion of the comfortable, lounge type furniture out of the public areas of our Main Library in downtown Tampa.

Again note that one attempted solution to Tampa's problem involves almost no money. Simply making the library a less attractive setting for the behavior of the offensive patrons helps control the problem. Of course, this action makes the library a little less attractive for the "normal" patron as well. But these patrons probably are willing to trade comfortable furniture for a less disruptive library.

The Grand Rapids (Michigan) Public Library also reported that problem patrons were among its most serious problems, as did another midwestern library.

> Exposures and other disruptive behaviors probably rank as the second most frequently reported problem (disruptive behaviors are generally caused by alcohol consumption but [we] have also ones originating in an emotional imbalance).
>
> Transients who are drunk or obviously high on something (drugs). Patrons who are disturbed mentally.

For most of the major libraries that did not specify problem patrons as their most serious problem, some type of theft was of the most concern. These acts ranged from break-ins involving major thefts of property and money to petty thefts affecting both staff and patrons. One major midwestern library indicated that its major problem was "breaking and entering in branch libraries at night, with theft of typewriters, lawn mowers, snow blowers, and other easily disposable items and equipment, and money from copying machines or change funds."

These thefts were dealt with in several different ways, some involving expensive security equipment; others were low-cost items. "[We] have electronic security systems monitored by a central office in all branches. Police are called when a break-in occurs. Some intruders have been apprehended and prosecuted and jailed. Police do not always arrive in time to catch the intruder."

Earlier in the year some research was carried out for the school systems in the same city as quoted above. One of their major problems turned out to be break-ins to buildings and theft of equipment. This points out the similarities between public schools and public libraries with regard to risk factors related to crime.

Similar problems were reported by a second midwestern library. In this case not only were break-ins a problem, but a rash of arson cases accompanied many of the intrusions. Librarians in this system attempted to deal with their problem in much the same way.

> We have installed electronic security systems in all branches and the main library with exterior and interior detectors. In addition, we installed fire detection systems in all agencies of the system which, by the way, failed to detect a serious arson fire which extensively damaged one branch. The detection systems seem to have prevented some loss from break-ins. They do, however, present numerous problems from false alarms and faulty equipment.

The theft of equipment can be very disruptive to the everyday functioning of the institution. Even if the risks are known by the staff, action to deter these thefts cannot always be initiated, or so it is often believed:

"Lack of funds prevents us from making equipment within the branches more secure. Equipment is an inviting target for theft or break-ins. Each branch has prepared a checklist of things to be done to secure the branch for evening closing. This has prevented oversights from occurring when substitutes are staffing branches."

A southwestern library that did not wish to be identified indicated that theft of library materials and equipment was the most serious problem encountered. In that system guards were used at the exits, but they did not have the right to search individuals who might be hiding materials in their clothing and such. The respondent indicated that attempts to secure funding for a theft detection system had been denied several times. Book theft is, of course, a problem in many large and small libraries. As we have seen, larger libraries are more likely to have book theft detection systems, which greatly reduce the number of thefts. But not all major libraries have these systems in place.

> In the absence of an automated circulation or theft system (we are in the process of installing one) it is impossible to estimate our loss rate for library materials through theft, vandalism, or overdues. However, losses do seriously affect our ability to provide good service to our community.
>
> At the central library, unruly patrons are a major problem. . . . Book loss through theft and non-return of borrowed books is a serious problem also.
>
> We have uniformed security guards in the building during public hours. They can communicate with each other by two-way radios. They patrol the building in a prearranged manner and are available to staff on sight or by telephone. One guard mans the library exit area where patrons must display library materials to the guard on leaving the building. A bell sounds and one's exit from the building is barred if an attempt is made to remove books secretly from the building.

Losses through theft impact on individuals as well as the library. Personal property often is the principal target.

> Theft of patron and staff property (e.g., bicycles, purses, cameras, etc.) is the most frequent problem we encounter.
>
> Theft of employee and patron personal property, especially handbags and briefcases, by "professional" thieves. [We] increased security officer patrols, identification of likely suspects, more locked doors, desks, and cabinets; more reminding of patrons to watch their belongings.

The problems are as varied as are the solutions. Many libraries use a combination of low-cost and more expensive security measures. As we shall see later in this chapter, some of the most effective programs for reducing several types of crime are the low-cost, less sophisticated methods. Book theft, however, is most effectively handled in high-volume libraries with theft detection systems.

CRIME PREVENTION PROGRAMS

The study of crime prevention can be approached in many ways. Rather than focusing on the specific type of crime that is a problem, the institution may point up solutions by examining the possible weak points in its security.

Protecting a public institution (or any other setting) involves securing several possible weak points: (1) property lines, (2) possible entry points, (3) interior space, both general and specific, and (4) multiple points. Here we will examine security items that fall under the heading of hardware or equipment. Other security measures are discussed later under "Low-Cost Protection." Keep in mind, however, that not all hardware is costly, and even expensive items may become cost-effective in a short time depending on the magnitude of losses prevented.

Property Line Protection

Burglary, like most other crimes, is a crime of opportunity. If the opportunity for a successful burglary is minimized, such crimes are likely to be reduced. Security procedures reduce easy opportunities.

Property line protection refers to security measures that act as a physical or psychological barrier to the property itself. In most public institutions, these barriers do not keep people out completely as, for instance, one might find at a military installation. Rather they define the property lines in a way that reminds people that they are entering a protected area. The use of a fence or a wall rarely keeps intruders out, but it does let them know that they are in an area under control. This becomes most apparent when the facility is not open to the public at certain hours and the gate can be closed. Potential intruders must first make the decision to violate the boundary protection before they can even have access to the building. For some, this may be the added deterrent that makes the building an uninviting choice for their illegal activities. Keeping potential offenders away from the building may help to control vandalism as well as illegal entry.

Any perimeter security should not detract from other security programs. If police patrol coverage has been arranged, it is important that those on patrol have a clear view of the facility. High or solid fences or walls prevent easy surveillance. An attractive but thorny row of hedges may deter some unwanted entry. But be careful to consider legitimate users of the library. Installing fences, walls, hedges, and so on should not increase their risk of injury.

Several survey respondents indicated that they had contracted with security firms for guard dog coverage. These dogs can protect either the perimeter or the interior. In either case care must be taken to protect legitimate staff and users. Dogs can be trained to protect a site in several ways. Some are considered "attack" dogs who will charge either on command or on sighting an intruder; others are primarily watchdogs who serve as a noisy alarm when intruders are present. They also will frighten off many potential thieves and vandals. A sign warning intruders of guard dogs may be effective, particularly against nonprofessional criminals.

Proper lighting outside the facility can be an exceptionally valuable crime deterrent. Any new lighting being installed to improve visibility should be vandal-resistant. Lighting should focus on both the property around the building and the building itself, particularly possible entry points. Some of the newer types of security lighting require less maintenance and energy and provide more light. However, the cost of these systems may be substantially higher than conventional lighting.

Security personnel can control property lines effectively. Once again, the cost of such programs would have to be justified by the savings realized through crime prevention. Whether to use in-house or contracted guards is discussed below. One advanatage of security personnel is that they can provide multiple point coverage as well as perimeter protection. If these services are too costly, it may be possible to contract along with other public institutions for package coverage on a cost-sharing basis.

Protection of Entry Points

The protection of entry points should be extended beyond normal entry sites such as doors to include all possible entry points. These typically include windows, fire escapes, skylights, vents, and ducts. The most common illegal entry point is a door, so special attention should be paid to locks and door hinges. Doors that use a "key in the lock" mechanism are among the easiest for the intruder to open, either by "picking" or by breaking the lock. Deadbolt and newer versions of combination locks are an improvement over keyhole systems. Combination locks also help to reduce unauthorized entry by staff if the combination is not distributed freely. The construction of doors should be strong enough to resist the kinds of damage that facilitate entry. If door hinges are accessible from the outside, they can be altered to increase security. Crime prevention officers in the local police department will usually be willing to demonstrate this and other prevention techniques.

If there is a problem with access to areas containing exceptionally valuable or sensitive materials, some type of access control is essential. The use of cardkeys will restrict unauthorized personnel and provide a record of all legitimate entrances and exits. Even more foolproof (since cards can be lost, stolen, or sold) is the use of a hand- or fingerprint identifier. The fingerprint or handprint of the staff member seeking entry is automatically compared with the records stored in the system's microcomputer before access is granted to the secured area. The most likely need for such a costly system would be in rare book areas or other such locales.

In addition to locking systems, various types of intrusion alarms can be valuable. They function in different ways. A local alarm is activated only at the site, and response depends on direct observation by staff, citizen, or police. Alarms also may be sent to a privately owned central monitoring station and through it to police. Systems also can be installed that directly signal the police either by automatic direct dialing or by a monitored silent alarm. Local police can advise about availability and maintenance costs of these direct systems.

Two of the more common types of entry protection systems involve the use of thin metallic foil on vulnerable windows and contact switches on doors. When doors or windows are opened, the electronic or magnetic field is broken, triggering the alarm.

Some special problems should be noted about securing windows. Windows are easily broken and forced open. Alarms would indicate when this has occurred and would aid in scaring off or apprehending some offenders. But trying to prevent breakage and entry may be preferable. Installing some type of nonbreakable or break-resistant glass may be effective. However, keep in mind that a nonbreakable window also may prevent insiders from getting out in case of emergency. Be sure that adequate exits are available in case of fire or other danger. Similarly, improving the locking system on outside windows should be considered. In high-crime areas, bars or grates, although unattractive, may be useful. Skylights can be protected in similar ways.

Protecting Interior Locations

Securing the interior of the library should focus on both a general type of protection as well as a plan for specific critical areas. A variety of crimes may be a problem, including burglary, robbery, theft, vandalism and mutilation, and assault. Perimeter and entry protection can function as a first line of defense. If these security measures are not in place or not functioning properly, internal protection becomes even more critical. In the library, internal protection is important to protect against those who are in the building during normal operating hours as well as against those in the building when they should not be. Protection from employee crimes also may be increased with proper use of interior security.

A full range of alarm systems is available for interior protection, including motion detection, photoelectric, audio, weight-sensitive, and vibration systems. Each operates by detecting a change in the conditions within the specified area. Changes of sufficient magnitude activate the system, which in turn triggers the alarm (noise, silent, or automatic dialing).

Motion detection systems usually rely on either ultrasonic waves that are picked up by a receiver and if interrupted change the signal, or radio frequency waves, which operate the same way. Care should be taken to be sure that display items do not cause an alarm because of their motion. Decorative mobiles have been known to trigger false alarms. Photoelectric systems operate with an invisible beam of light received by a target component of the system. If the beam is deflected from the target, the alarm is activated. Mirrors can transmit the beam in patterns other than a straight line. Audio or sonic alarms depend on noise to activate the system. Sensitive receivers pick up noises of an intruder, but ignore sounds of nonthreatening origin, such as wind, fans, and so on. The weight-sensitive or pressure alarms are activated when pressure is placed on the object (carpet, mat, and so on) concealing the sensor. Vibration alarms typically are attched directly to high-risk objects. Any movement of these objects sets off the warning.

In addition to an alarm system, several other security programs should be considered for interior protection. Adequate lighting is crucial in the prevention of some crimes. Both the exterior and interior should be adequately lighted. After hours, a combination of interior lighting and clear visibility of the interior from the outside is valuable. There is one exception to the value of good lighting. If the problems are being caused by amateurs or juveniles, the absence of lighting can be effective as long as the interior of the building is visible from the outside (through windows and the like). Many intruders prefer not to enter a totally dark and unknown setting because the light that they will have to use inside may attract attention.

There is growing use of closed circuit surveillance in many public and private institutions. Costs can be high, but the value of the systems in deterring, detecting, and catching offenders is also high. For a maximum deterrent effect, use of the system has to be publicized. Decals, visible cameras (interspersed with dummies in some locations), and actual monitors do this well. Recent developments in the use of low-light lenses assist in the adequate surveillance of darker areas. Another recent improvement to the closed-circuit system, which uses a guard to monitor one or several locations, is the digital analysis of the images. Computer analysis of the signals from the cameras can identify any unusual changes with far greater accuracy than the human observer. However, the guard monitoring the system can perform other functions as well.

There has been some controversy surrounding the use of camera surveillance in public places (see Figure 17).

Video Monitor System Draws Public Ire

The Arlington Heights Memorial Library, Illinois, has installed five small TV monitors to watch over various hard-to-supervise areas of the library. The TV screens are at the front desk and allow staff members to keep an eye on the lower lobby and the rear of the adult section, which is obscured by stacks.

Reactions of patrons are reported as mixed, says the *Nor'easter*, newsletter of the North Suburban Library System. While most patrons have accepted the system with little comment, and the staff likes its convenience, a few patrons reacted with great indignation to the "peeping Toms at the library" and "Big Brother." The controversy was aired on CBS television in the middle of October.

The TV equipment, according to director Harold Ard, cost about $5000, with practically no maintenance costs foreseen. He expects opposition to die down eventually.

Video Monitor OK'd by Illinois Library

The library board of Arlington Heights Memorial Library, Illinois, has voted four to one to keep a controversial video monitoring system which has raised a great deal of adverse comment in local news media. Harold J. Ard, executive librarian, updated *LJ*'s coverage (*LJ*, December 1, p. 4335) with a summary of the reasons for the decision.

They were: although it does not replace the night monitor, it aids him in doing an effective job; it is helpful during the day when there is no monitor on duty; it prevents "making a premature judgment"; and it does perform its main function of providing surveillance of areas farthest from the main desk.

Also: the "large silent majority" of patrons appreciate any means of controlling library atmosphere, complaints only coming at board meetings; the system has a "psychological effect in deterring would-be troublemakers"; with a probable life of ten years the per year cost for this added protection will be very low. A final reason, said Ard, was "to be among the first in the library field to try this innovative means of control."

■ Figure 17 From *Library Journal*, December 1, 1969, p. 4335, and January 15, 1970, p. 113.

Whether or not a general interior security system is used, there still may be a need for some security at specific risk points. Closed-circuit television naturally would include such points as exits, storage areas, back stacks, and offices, but few libraries use such expensive techniques. What else can be done to help secure specific settings? The first priority is to identify the potential risk areas (discussed in more detail later in this chapter). In general terms, most libraries have to protect their staff and materials. Staff is most vulnerable either in isolated areas or around valuable materials. Materials are most vulnerable when they are easily taken from their original setting and easily removed from the building. Display cases should be properly locked and if possible made of break-resistant materials. Sliding doors on these cases should be fitted with adequate locks, and the tops of the cases, if removable, should be locked or fastened. The undersides of display cases should be examined for easy access. If small valuable materials are being kept in the library, the use of a fire- and burglar-resistant safe should be considered.

The major problem involving theft in most libraries centers around book theft. Book theft detection systems are, of course, the most common "hardware" solution to the problem. In general, this involves the protection of a critical point—the exit. Exits can be protected automatically or manually. In either case the added surveillance makes it more difficult to successfully remove materials without being detected. As was noted in our earlier discussion of problems with theft detectors, patrons sometimes attempt to circumvent these systems. However, most reports indicate that the systems are effective in reducing book thefts.

Multiple Point Protection

Security programs are generally most effective if several or all of the areas discussed above are protected. Many general techniques can ensure this. The use of closed-circuit cameras can be extended to almost any location in or around the facility. Security personnel can be posted to give adequate coverage in any or all of the areas. Security guards should be thought of as a crime prevention component of a security program. In contrast, local police often come into the picture after the episode has occurred. Police can, however, help prevent crime through increased patrols, crime prevention training, and effective apprehension of offenders who might repeat or encourage others to commit more crime against the library.

Guards work full time for their employer and thus can be more effective than the occasional presence of local police. But the institution will pay for this benefit. Assuming an assessment has been made and the use of security guards has been recommended, several choices have to be made. The options of in-house and contract services for guards must be examined. To assist in making this choice, the current and anticipated needs of the institution should be assessed. What is expected of the security guards? What are the most essential needs and the major problems?

According to Schindler, security guards can be expected to provide a variety of services if needed.[6] These include:

142 □ CRIME IN THE LIBRARY

1. Access control
2. Control of removal of items
3. Fire watch
4. Crowd control
5. Information and assistance
6. Inspection of safety and fire fighting equipment
7. Control of fire evacuation
8. Observation of employee activity
9. Patrol of premises
10. Parking lot control
11. Lock up
12. Setting and testing of alarm systems
13. Building evacuation during emergencies such as bomb threats
14. Observation
15. Reports covering observations in all phases of operations

Schindler's list covers both a variety of activities and a variety of locations in and around the library. Several suggestions about what guards should not be expected to do are mentioned as well, such as that guards should not perform janitorial duties, do book shelving, discipline employees, or any other activities that lower the esteem of the guards in the eyes of observers (see Figure 18).

Whether to hire and train your own security personnel or to contract for the services is not an easy decision. As suggested by Robert Gallati in his

---

Stabbing Incident at NYPL

In recent years libraries have become increasingly concerned with the need for protecting people in libraries. Guards are considered to be almost mandatory, especially in urban libraries. A recent incident at the New York Public Library dramatizes how important the protection provided by a guard can be. According to a report in New York's *Daily News*, a mental patient out on a pass from the New York State Manhattan Psychiatric Center on Wards Island pulled out a knife for no apparent reason and assaulted another patron at NYPL's North Hall reading room. Library guard William Normoyle raced to the scene and subdued the mental patient, who was sent to Bellevue Hospital's Psychiatric unit for observation. The victim of the stabbing had to be hospitalized.

■ Figure 18 From *Library Journal*, June 15, 1979, p. 1302.

book on private security,[7] there are advantages and disadvantages to each approach:

1. Advantages of proprietary guards: a. More loyal to the company; b. Career-oriented, less likely to quit; c. Can be fashioned to your own mold; d. Know the territory better; e. May be a source of pride for the company.

2. Advantages of contractual guards: a. Flexibility in terms of numbers of guards, hours worked, and getting rid of "foul balls"; b. Usually there are a full array of specialists that you can count on for unusual situations; c. Usually cost less per person than proprietary personnel with their fringe benefits and so on; d. Eliminate the need for managerial chores such as selecting, training, uniforming, supervising, and so on; e. Particularly good for undercover work where proprietary personnel would be likely to be recognized; f. Are more likely to be objective in their treatment of situations since they have no permanent ties.

3. Disadvantages of proprietary guards: a. More expensive; b. May not have specialist expertise or be able to operate undercover; c. Require time and effort to select, train, uniform, and supervise; d. Difficult to discharge if it is warranted; if there is a union it may be very traumatic; e. May not be objective about their work because of friendships and so on; f. More likely to be in collusion with other employees they get to know well.

4. Disadvantages of contractual forces: a. No feeling of loyalty or special concern for the company; b. Are not career-oriented and will most likely do only as much as they are "pushed" to do; c. Generally not as qualified as proprietary personnel, often hired at minimum wage scale; d. Receive very generic training if at all, and may not be able to apply it to specific situations; e. Often their appearance and conduct reflect poorly on the company; f. May become involved in theft because of their low wages and lack of stability as casual employees.

Gallati claims that even this extensive list is not complete. Depending on the specific situation, other criteria may become important considerations for the administrator. These advantages and disadvantages were designed with a company in mind. Most apply as well to the library, but local priorities such as service to the public may shed a different light on this range of suggestions.

LOW-COST PROTECTION

Much earlier it was suggested that libraries had a good deal in common with other public institutions such as schools and museums. Many of these institutions generally have been more security conscious than have libraries. Schools, for example, went through a period in the 1970s of intensive research on problems of crime, which resulted in programs to control the problems. Many school programs are directly applicable to libraries. Similarly, many of the security programs now in retail establishments can fit the needs of the library with only minor changes. In this section, we review several types of security programs that have been used successfully, but typically not in libraries, as well as some designed specifically for libraries.

General Programs

Different crime and disruption problems naturally require different types of crime prevention programs. If theft is a problem, particularly if employees or ex-employees may be suspected, some control over lock and key seems necessary. If assault is a concern, personal safety precautions may be warranted. Several low-cost programs are effective against a variety of crimes. Let us examine them and then look at programs that tend to focus on particular crime problems.

VISIBILITY ENHANCEMENT. A thorough examination of the library's physical layout may reveal an inadequate view or surveillance of some risk areas. Visibility enhancement increases the possibility of observing undesirable acts. Attempts to conceal or mutilate materials might be deterred if the potential offender has difficulty finding a private spot to do so. Most deviant sexual behavior will not be carried out if detection or interruption is likely. And burglary is not as apt to occur if there is clear vision into the library.

Many of the problems described by librarians from major and smaller libraries involve the actions of disruptive patrons, as well as theft and mutilation. Each of these is facilitated by privacy. If the potential offender believes that he or she is not likely to be observed, the act is more likely to occur. Enhancing visibility within the library can, therefore, deter many of these acts. The use of wide-area mirrors in commercial establishments, for instance, is now commonplace. These visual aids can also be put to good use in the library setting. They allow one person to maintain some visual coverage of areas that might otherwise be hidden, and they are of particular value to a librarian working alone in the building who must be in one place while disruptive activity might be taking place somewhere else. (The wisdom of working alone under such circumstances should, of course, be questioned.) These highly visible mirrors also serve as a deterrent to potential offenders who become concerned about detection.

Enhanced visibility can be achieved by rearranging shelving, files, displays, and office furniture. With less space to survey, smaller institutions would find this tactic fairly easy to put into practice. Displays should be arranged so that missing items can be readily spotted. Whenever structural changes are being contemplated or new building is undertaken, a thorough analysis of security should be included as part of the architectural planning.

Often improved security can be had without additional cost or sacrifice of basic design. For example, running stacks in one direction gives greater and easier visibility than a more complex arrangement. Some libraries leave gaps in their shelving; either a whole row at eye level is left out or peepholes are scattered about within the stacks. Both increase visibility of otherwise isolated areas. All study and browsing areas should be kept as open as possible. Here again, a wide-angle or even a one-way mirror can allow better protection of patron, staff, and materials.

The personal safety of staff working alone or in isolated areas can be increased by providing easy visibility of the work area. Private offices in the small library do afford privacy, but they also afford opportunity for crime. An interior office window allows the staff member to keep an eye on what is going on in the building, and also allows patrons to keep watch for suspicious activity in the office. Usually there is no increased risk caused by having a staff member visible in the office. The danger to an employee alone in the building would not be aggravated by increased visibility into the office area.

As noted earlier, visibility from the street can be important. Criminals do not like to operate when there is likelihood of detection. Any technique that increases visibility within and into the institution is of value. And do not neglect the area around the library that is used by staff and patrons. Minimizing blind spots near the building and in parking lots not only makes honest patrons and staff feel more secure, but actually increases the safety of these areas.

POLICE PATROL AND DROP-IN. An effective and low-cost program to deter theft and vandalism after hours is the random patrol of police near or in the building. Empty libraries are prime targets for thieves and vandals. Security personnel would deter much of this crime, but they may be prohibitively expensive for most libraries. The alternative may be available right in the community at the police department.

Many police departments require their officers on patrol or answering calls to prepare a detailed report of their activities. The standard procedure is often to return to the station to complete the paperwork before resuming patrol duty. Several public school systems have a setup with local police in which the school provides a "night office" in the building for the use of officers on patrol. Libraries could do the same. Rather than returning to the station, officers on duty could drop into the library on a random basis to prepare their reports. Police would remain in contact with the station before going out on the next call. The presence of police would be unpredictable, making it very undesirable for anyone to attempt to break into or vandalize the building. Cost is low and protection is high.

Reports from areas where this program has been tried have been favorable. Any inappropriate behavior by police in the building, although unlikely, would be noticeable to administrators monitoring the effectiveness of the program.

If the drop-in program is not appropriate or feasible, increasing patrol coverage by police can be effective. This works best when coverage is not scheduled on a regular basis that could be determined by potential offenders. The major exception to unplanned patrol coverage is during closing hours. Departing staff and patrons are better protected if police patrols are visible in the area during closing times. These patrols could be coordinated with a lockup procedure if the risk is great enough. Police would accompany the lone staff member of the small library as he or she secures the building and goes to the parking area.

PROSECUTION POLICY. What is likely to happen if a staff member is caught committing some minor crime? Consider for a moment the possibility that an employee has been apprehended stealing a couple of books or some petty cash. What if a patron does the same thing or rips out several pages from an art book? When a crime is serious enough (as defined by local administrators), some type of formal action will be taken in most cases. But what are those limits? They should be defined for the institution, perhaps in consultation with local police and prosecutors. Whatever policy is established should be explained to all employees and even posted for those patrons who might be considering offensive actions.

Prosecution is not always a low-cost option. However, it tends to have such a strong deterrent effect, both on the immediate offender and others who become aware of the case, that it can be cost-effective. It is important to apply whatever policy is developed in a consistent manner. This does not mean that exceptions cannot be made in individual cases, but rather that the normal range of cases will be handled in the normal manner.

Prosecution should be considered as an integral part of any crime prevention program. Most criminals weigh both the likelihood of being caught and the likelihood of being prosecuted and punished when picking targets. There are too many stories of libraries being perceived as "good pickings" because of ample opportunity for crime and a low likelihood of prosecution (see Figure 19).

Programs for Specific Crimes

THEFT BY OUTSIDERS. The range of theft that can plague the library is mind-boggling. There is theft of books, money, materials, audiovisual

LAPL Lowers the Boom on Book Thefts

The Los Angeles Public Library recently took an overambitious acquirer of its books to court after repossessing 554 books worth $5,238 which he had squirreled away. The judge gave the culprit a $250 fine and three years probation.

LAPL maintains a force of four field investigators who keep busy going after library materials held over six weeks overdue. Last year they brought back 7,716 books valued at $42,706, in some cases also spotting stolen books while going after overdues.

■ Figure 19 From *Library Journal,* January 1, 1970, p. 20.

---

equipment, antiques, briefcases, and on and on. Sometimes these thefts occur during open hours by people who walk in the front door. Sometimes these and other types of theft involve breaking and entering when the library is closed.

The general programs already described should help to prevent some thefts. An additional low-cost program that can be effective, particularly during regular hours, is to increase control over movement within the facility. Movement controls should include procedures designed to monitor access to the facility, movement within the library, and exit from the building. Two plans may be necessary—one for patrons and one for staff. Initially, a walking inventory of the facility should take place, noting all locations that patrons and possibly staff should *not* have access to. For patrons this would typically include offices, storage rooms, sites where cash and keys are kept, the staff lounge, processing areas, and receiving areas. Restricted areas for the staff may be determined on an employee-category or a case-by-case basis.

It might help for this inventory to think of the library as a store. Customers are desired, but their actions are controlled. They should have full access to browse through the merchandise without damaging or pilfering. On the other hand, there are many locations within the "store" where they would be in the way or a danger to security. In an actual store, these off-limit areas are clearly marked, often with physical barriers as well as signs. After conducting business, customers are expected to leave in an orderly manner through whatever check-out routes are specified. Control over merchandise is exercised at these points. This is not to suggest that library patrons should be made to feel like they are in a supermarket or a shoe store; however, it is a good idea for the staff to keep in mind the movement controls that such businesses use.

How can this be accomplished at little expense? Most libraries already have some movement controls. Those with book detection systems check merchandise before patrons exit. Libraries without automated systems should be sure that all patrons must at least pass by a staff member before leaving. The easiest way for patrons to steal materials is to conceal them on the person or in belongings when they can use an exit where they will not encounter a staff member. Even libraries staffed by one person can arrange the work area so that departing patrons cannot get to the door without some human contact. This will deter most patrons, particularly in those small libraries where everybody tends to know one another. If some work areas are not in office-type settings, access can be controlled by using counters or cubicles that fasten when the employee leaves and must be opened with a key before going back in. Personal belongings should not be left in clear view in these areas.

Normal patron traffic patterns should be examined. If some areas in the library attract only an occasional patron or staff member, and if it is not possible to somehow increase surveillance there, then rearranging shelves or other facilities can increase the use of the area. If there is adequate use, many of the actions that require privacy become more risky. Other isolated areas such as rest rooms may require restricted access. In addition, these rest rooms should not be located, if possible, in isolated areas of the building. Safety is compromised when legitimate patrons and staff have to go "downstairs and around the corner," "out in the back hall," or "up to the third floor behind the auto repair manuals."

Movement control can be extended to areas outside the building as well. Safe, well-lighted paths to the parking areas or street and restricted access to back doors and receiving areas will be helpful.

If theft problems are thought to be the result of employee or ex-employee activities, enhanced lock and key control is essential. A simple but rather costly approach is to change all the locks in the institution and all the branches. To avoid the expense of a total replacement program, the institution may be able to achieve the same level of security by exchanging locks. Note the following procedure:

> Maintaining control over keys is a major problem in building security. Administrators are concerned with providing sufficient access to areas in and about the school for personnel who must work in these areas. However, administrators are also concerned that the lack of proper issuance procedures and care in handling keys will constitute a hazard to the security of the building. . . . Staff need frequent access to storage and audiovisual supply rooms. However, individual carelessness is often cited by school security personnel as the major reason for lost and/or misplaced keys to these vital areas and subsequent property loss. According to Charles O'Toole, Chief of Security for the Seattle Public Schools, the "period of credibility for any lock and key system averages from two to five years. Within this timeframe, or as the need arises, the lock and

key system for any school district should be changed. Accomplishing this task can be quite expensive. . . . In the State of Washington, several school systems participate in a lock and key exchange program. Periodically, neighboring districts exchange lock cores and/or combination locks to lockers along with all master keys and combination locks. This type of program increases the security and credibility of the lock and key system in these districts and is cost effective."[8]

A similar type of exchange can be operated between libraries in neighboring communities or between the branches within a system. This program helps ensure that only authorized personnel have access to sensitive areas or areas with high value materials. The actual exchange can often be made by the maintenance staff of the institution or by a locksmith if necessary. In either case, costs for new materials are virtually nonexistent. Once the new program is in place, the number of employees with keys or access to keys should be kept to a minimum.

Maintaining security over the keys themselves is as important as the distribution process. Keys should be centrally controlled and inventoried so that missing items are noted quickly. Basically, keys should be issued only on a need basis. Controls should include coding keys so they cannot be easily matched with corresponding locks by unauthorized personnel. All keys should be stamped "Do Not Duplicate." Reputable locksmiths will honor this request. Whenever an employee leaves voluntarily or otherwise, all keys assigned to that person should be accounted for. The centralized and secure setting for duplicate keys should be an area from which the public and if possible most employees are restricted (see Figure 20).

Another inexpensive program to combat employee theft is a two-pronged focus on employee screening and morale. Before anyone is hired, some type of background check should be made. All too often, because of time or budget limitations, administrators responsible for hiring tend to ignore these necessary procedures. Of course, if the applicant is someone who is known to the administrator, the check can be more superficial. But

Los Angeles Library Staffer Accused of Major Theft

A missing persons alert led police to the apartment of a Los Angeles Public Library staff member where they discovered a stockpile of some 10,000 books stacked from floor to ceiling.

Glenn Swartz, currently facing criminal charges, had lived in the apartment for 22 years. According to witnesses it was common to see him toting bags of books, even several years before he went to work for the library.

■ Figure 20 From *Library Journal*, December 1, 1982, p. 2212.

at the very least, a check with a former employer should be made even in those cases.

A comprehensive employment application not only lists previous experiences and current skills, but also references who can be contacted. References should be contacted in writing or by telephone. Phone calls are more likely to elicit a response because they are quick and leave no written record, which generally prompts the individual to give a more honest evaluation of strengths and weaknesses. Any derogatory information should be double-checked to protect the applicant.

Take particular note of an applicant who does not provide references from a previous place of employment. However, keep in mind that an unsatisfactory situation may have been the result of something the applicant did or failed to do, but it may also indicate something about the employer or work situation.

In typical cases, the applicant's previous employment history should be traced back at least several years. Credit checks may reveal unusual pressures that might encourage dishonest behavior. Will the salary being offered provide enough relief from other financial pressures? If not, the applicant should not necessarily be rejected but rather restricted at first from activities that provide easy opportunity for theft.

To maintain the efficiency and commitment of this carefully selected staff, administrators should pay attention to employee morale. Naturally, the larger the staff, the more difficult it is to be in touch with the problems of each one. Yet we know that as morale declines, various types of losses tend to increase. This includes losses due to absenteeism, wasted time on the job, and actual thefts. Recall that one of the keys to an effective prosecution policy is that it be fairly and objectively applied. All employee policies should be perceived by the staff in this way. Any disciplinary as well as incentive and promotion policies should be clearly defined and fairly applied.

Wage equity is crucial. If employees feel that they are being paid less than they deserve in comparison with others on the staff, satisfaction drops markedly and motivation to "get even" with the institution increases. Periodic reviews of wage structures can be beneficial in spotting problems before they become acute.

A system of grievance communication should be worked out. Employees should be told how to air their problems through proper channels and shown how these concerns are attended to. A solution to the problem may not be as important initially as is the perception that the issue is given proper attention. Institutional policies about theft and other crimes should be clearly spelled out, leaving no doubt in the minds of employees about what will happen if infractions are discovered.

The importance of preventing crime by patrons and others should be stressed. Employees usually are responsive to requests for cooperation when it has been pointed out that cooperation not only helps ensure their own safety, but also helps to maintain the operating budget at reasonable levels. Savings resulting from employee initiatives in preventing crime could be used to improve working conditions, salaries, or benefits. This becomes an added incentive for employees to work toward a crime-free environment.

MUTILATION OF MATERIALS. Information noted in earlier chapters makes it clear that mutilation of materials is a serious and costly problem in all kinds of libraries. Several of the low-cost programs that have been described will help control mutilation—increased visibility, use of security guards, an evident prosecution program, and others. Lawler describes a "practical plan of attack" for controlling theft and mutilation that meets the criteria of being low cost and workable. Although the focus here is on an academic library, most of the points apply equally well in the public library setting. Lawler makes nine recommendations, including:

Education and publicity: alert users to costs of the problem

Enlisting aid: use of volunteers during busy times

Staff cooperation with users

Adequate and possibly subsidized copying facilities

Adequate circulation policies

Realistic policy for reserve material

Well-publicized penalties for mutilation

Inspection of backpacks, parcels, etc. at exit

Consistent application of penalties[9]

According to Lawler, none of these suggestions alone will solve the problem and even the combined effort is "no guarantee of success." But these options coupled with several additional tactics described earlier may provide enough of a reduction in destruction to be cost-effective. Specifically, the prompt repair of mutilated materials should be undertaken. Once a journal or book is damaged, it tends to stimulate similar behavior by other readers. At the same time, an assessment of the most common targets in the institution can be made. This may help to identify areas where there is a need for tighter controls, additional surveillance, or more copies placed on reserve, if the collection is being used for academic purposes (see Figure 21).

University of Nebraska Reports Sharp Rise in Mutilation

The University of Nebraska at Omaha reports a startling rise in the mutilation and theft of library materials in just one year: over 1,100 pages from magazines have had to be replaced since January 1981 and 672 complete issues had to be ordered to replace magazines that had been stolen or destroyed. A task force of faculty and staff was formed to examine the problem and find a cure.

In a letter to inform students and faculty, UN's Technical Services Chairperson Carroll Varner identified the top targets for mutilation, each losing up to 90 pages: *Journal of Criminal Law, Journal of Family Issues, American Sociological Review, Academy of Management Journal, Banking Law Journal, Audubon, Food Technology, Environmental Psychology, American Film,* and *Smith College Studies in Social Work.* This list includes only those magazines which are bound in paper for preservation, not those already microfilmed. Prior to the study UNO had assumed that its more scholarly journals were not being mutilated to this degree.

To call attention to the problem. UNO launched a campaign to highlight the problem. It mounted an exhibit of mutilated materials, including books with the entire contents ripped from their covers and magazines torn in half. Signs posted in the library noted that "Mutilation or theft of library materials is punishable under sections 28–511 and 28–519 of the Revised Statutes of Nebraska." Staff were briefed on what to do should they encounter a thief or vandal.

Noting that each article costs about $3 to replace, Varner urged faculty to help stop the crime wave by asking for photocopies "well before" giving the class the reading assignment and discussing openly with students the problem of crime in the stacks.

■ Figure 21 From *Library Journal*, December 1, 1982, p. 2212.

PROBLEM PATRONS. Assume for the moment that the major concern in this area is with nonviolent but aberrant patrons who use the library as a haven. Assume also that honest efforts have been made to control, modify, or remove those patrons and that for any number of reasons, such efforts have been less than a total success. At such a point a different approach may be appropriate. Since these patrons in need of services are "hanging around" the library, why not provide the services that they need? That is, encourage a professional from an appropriate social agency to set up shop in the library. This would serve several functions. Initially, it would demonstrate without doubt the magnitude of the problem experienced by staff and patron. Second, it would allow the mental health professional access to a large number of clients in need of care, supervision, or therapy. This would free the library staff from the role of monitor and lookout. Finally, patrons could gradually be diverted from the library to other more appropriate settings without being thrown out into the streets from which they are trying to escape.

This idea does not suggest that libraries become mental health centers for the community. Rather, if conventional approaches do not work and there is a reluctance to call in police, then bringing in someone trained and in part responsible for the problem may be effective. In cases where the library already is functioning as a drop-in center, the professional help may be of great aid. Space in the library could be set aside for this program, thus freeing other areas from these problem patrons. Attention should be given only to those patrons who use the library as their regular "safe place." New candidates should not be brought into the library but rather handled through normal channels. Those willing to seek help who are in the library regularly should respond to the agency professional. Those trying to avoid help will probably clear out of the library at the first sign of a case worker. But either outcome may be better for the library than the present situation.

Several respondents to the survey of major libraries indicated that they had tried to solve their problems with unusual patrons by rearranging the physical layout of the library. This was at least partially successful. Recall that suggestions included removing comfortable furniture from favored areas and placing the most popular newspapers in an area that allowed greater supervision and was out of the way. In addition, encouraging problem patrons to use areas in full view of the outside may provide added security by police patrolling the street. Also, restricting the comforts sought by these patrons may encourage them to go elsewhere. For example, access to the rest rooms could be by key, and any furniture in them that is conducive to napping could be removed. Changes in the physical arrangements could be coupled with stricter enforcement of rules (see Figure 22).

PROBLEMS WITH ASSAULT. In the early 1970s, teachers in New York City prepared a set of guidelines for protecting staff from assault. These suggestions are still valid today, not only for school personnel but for librarians as well. The implications are most evident for librarians working in school systems or with students in other settings.

> Don't be an early bird. Most of the "vicious attacks" in school buildings have occurred during the hour before school opens. . . . Some felons are early risers; others have not yet retired for the night before school opens. . . . Attacks by intruders: Most intruders fall into one of three categories: (1) armed robbers, (2) older kids, (3) irate parents. If an intruder suddenly enters your room, UFT recommends that you should "overcome the natural tendency to freeze at the approach of a menacing intruder." Get out of the room fast and

Director Says Rules a Key for Calm Library

By Bill Cantwell
Eagle-Tribune Writer

LAWRENCE—Changes in rules and the physical setup of the Public Library have taken a chunk out of vandalism and "disgusting behavior" patrons and workers have experienced there.

But library officials say unless they continue to enforce the changes, vandals may tear bathroom-stall doors down, rip apart chair cushions, break table legs and slash car tires.

Those are incidents that happened there frequently in the last year, according to Library Director Barbara DeYoung.

In September library officials reorganized materials and offices, vacating several corners of the second floor.

Youths began to congregate there loudly, while vandalism increased, Mrs. DeYoung said.

"The level of destruction was very high," she said. "There was dope dealing, loud music from radios, a security guard knocked down and severe, abusive language shouted across the floor at staff people, disgusting behavior."

Mrs. DeYoung said:

VANDALISM ranged from ripped chair cushions to a urinal being torn off the men's room wall.

CUSTODIANS now devote much of their time to repairing desks, chairs and damage to the plumbing in bathrooms.

VIOLENCE included threats to workers and patrons who asked youths to be quiet.

IN ONE INSTANCE, a teenager broke a bulletin board over a security guard's head while being ushered from the building for using abusive language.

Then came a big change: Library officials no longer allowed more than two people at a time for private reading in the corners, and cracked down on anyone disturbing the quiet atmosphere.

Students working on group projects can gather for discussions only in an open area with large tables located in the center of a room near a librarian's desk.

Library officials don't allow students in the facility during school hours to discourage truancy.

Anyone using the facility must present his library card whenever a librarian or other worker asks to see it, while security has been increased.

Library officials said the changes have produced some improvement, but are cautious not to get too secure.

"It's better, but you never know how long it's going to stay that way," Mrs. DeYoung said.

Some patrons said the changes have brought improvements, while others remain pessimistic.

"I frequent here usually twice a week," said Nick Carter, 372 Elm St. "I have seen some young fellows get pretty fresh in here. But I think it's quieted down. There might have been only a few kids who made it bad for the rest."

Several patrons refused to talk about library officials' charges of extreme loudness and threats from youths congregating in the building.

"These kids are smart," said a man who refused to be identified. "If they see my face (in a newspaper picture) they'll rip my tires."

■ Figure 22 From the *Eagle-Tribune* (Lawrence, Massachusetts), March 27, 1983.

yell for help. You are a sitting duck if you don't.... If you're attacked: Talk slowly; talk softly; avoid quick movements.... Many robbers (or assailants) are prone to gratuitous attacks. If attacked: go down with the first blow and stay down. Don't be alone! There is one cardinal rule for safety: never be alone, for any extended period of time, anywhere in the school. Even during lunchtime, it is dangerous to eat alone in the room. You may feel safe because the door is locked—but locks can be picked. More important: assault records show that when someone knocks, school personnel tend to open the door.[10]

How does a librarian in a small library make sure that he or she is not alone? A community-based institution can arrange for people to be in what otherwise might be an empty building. As a public institution, libraries offer many services. These could be expanded at little cost to the library to encourage building use by approved groups. An occupied library tends to be a safer library.

Many schools plagued by violence, vandalism, and assaults on staff and students in almost empty buildings have expanded programs during hours that typically are quiet. That is, the building can function in part as a social and service center for recognized groups in the area. Many of these groups are grateful for a safe and comfortable place to meet. Again, this is merely an extension of services that many libraries already offer. Even though there may be some increase in the cost of maintenance and energy, the advantages of having people in an otherwise quiet building should outweigh these costs. Safety will be improved and community relations should be boosted as well.

In addition, the use of the library as a community gathering place may allow other public institutions to reduce their operating costs. This savings in other areas should be pointed out during the next round of budget negotiations. A small fee could be charged to help offset the added maintenance costs. Groups using the facility should be informed of all relevant library policies regarding their behavior while in the building. One member of the group should be designated as the liaison with the library to ensure that adequate communications are maintained. Overall, a building that has people with strong community ties in it is a safer building than the unoccupied or nearly empty facility.

Once any of these low-cost programs is implemented by a library, flexibility should be stressed. After a program is started, review and revise the plans as needed.

DESIGNING A SECURITY PROGRAM

How can library administrators best secure facilities? Designing a good security program involves a five-step approach: devising a security checklist, making a risk assessment study, monitoring crime patterns, establishing a reporting procedure, and implementing the program.

Security Checklist

A security checklist is a general set of guidelines that works well in many similar settings. This one is geared to the library that has done little with security, the typical library in our study. Local conditions have to be taken into account to fill the gaps in the procedure. A good checklist might be based on seven components that have been shown to be related to problems of crime and disruption in libraries. Both the characteristics of the community and those of the institution can facilitate or deter crime. In this list, we have included those characteristics that may increase the risk of crime. This list may work as well in other public institutions.

The major categories of the security checklist include:

1. Location and community characteristics
    a. Know the crime rate in your community.
    b. Know the crime rate in your neighborhood.
    c. Know the kinds of crime that are common nearby.

    The following may increase the risk of crime:

    d. The library is far from a police station.
    e. The library is near a school.
    f. The library is near an agency serving indigents.
    g. The library is isolated from other buildings.
    h. An offender can approach the building without being seen.
2. Characteristics of the institution

    The following may increase the risk of crime:

    a. The library operates at night.
    b. Money is kept in the building at night.
    c. A staff member works alone.
    d. Items of high value are kept in the library.
    e. Signs are not posted describing penalties for crimes.
    f. Many teenage patrons are served.
3. Perimeter control
    a. Avoid or get rid of hidden locations outside.
    b. Avoid or get rid of hidden spots in the parking lot.
    c. The exterior of the library should be well-lit.
    d. Fences and shrubs should not block visibility.
    e. Police should patrol on an unpredictable schedule.
4. Entry control
    a. Door locks should be difficult to pick or damage.

b. Exposed hinges should be reinforced.
   c. Entry points should have adequate alarms.
   d. Windows should have security locks.
   e. The fire escape must be protected.
   f. Vents and ducts must be protected.
   g. Skylights must be protected.
   h. Patrons should not leave the building undetected.
   i. Keys should be marked "Do Not Duplicate."
   j. Consider break-resistant windows.
5. Interior space control
   a. Posters and displays should not block view from outside.
   b. Posters and displays should not block view of outside.
   c. Get rid of or avoid hidden spots within the building.
   d. Consider not allowing patrons to carry bags, etc.
   e. Keep all areas of library well-lit.
   f. Keep displays locked.
   g. Do not let employees have keys they do not need.
   h. Do not let people "hang out" in private locations.
   i. Consider limiting access to the rest rooms.
   j. Do not leave staff members alone on floors.
   k. Arrange stacks for maximum visibility.
   l. Have visibility of study areas.
   m. Arrange for peepholes in shelves.
   n. Control access to elevators.
   o. Avoid partition walls that can be climbed over.
   p. Keep all staff areas locked.
6. Management of materials and contents
   a. Keep cash out of patrons' reach.
   b. Cash container must be secure.
   c. Keep valuables in a locked room.
   d. Arrange displays so that missing items can be readily noticed.
   e. Check inventories often enough to detect ongoing theft.
   f. All desks should lock.
   g. Keep equipment bolted to desks or secured at night.
   h. Keep personal belongings in locked areas for the staff.
7. Personnel factors
   a. Develop a clear procedure for reporting crime.
   b. Train staff in crime prevention.
   c. Do not ignore minor thefts and other crimes.
   d. Develop a set of guidelines for prosecution.
   e. Do not hesitate to prosecute when necessary.
   f. Conduct thorough background and reference checks.
   g. Clearly state policies for acceptable employee behavior.

h. Do not ignore minor employee infractions.
i. Limit access to phone and supplies to essential staff.

Risk Assessment Study

The emphasis in the security checklist is on relatively low-cost security options, and it is designed primarily for libraries that have done little with security. Where do you go from there? The next step is a risk assessment study. Three questions should be considered part of a risk analysis: (1) What are the vulnerable locations within or around the library? Setting priorities for the treatment of these areas is important. (2) What is the likelihood of a problem actually occurring at one of these points? Not all vulnerable points are equally as likely to be targets for crime. For example, a piano and a display of antiques may be in the same area. The antiques are more likely to be stolen. It is, therefore, more important to secure the antiques. Generally, protecting items that have a high likelihood of theft or damage is more important than the protection of items less likely to be stolen. (3) What is the impact of the potential crime? That is, what would happen if a particular item were damaged or stolen? The best indicator of the impact is to consider the consequences for the institution. Some actions can have serious consequences; others have little effect. For example, the destruction of circulation or business records would have far more impact on the functioning of the institution than would the loss of a rare book. So even though the loss of a rare book is the more likely occurrence, the protection of the records (paper or software) may be more important. If there are any items that, even though not intrinsically valuable, are essential for the normal operation of the library, they should be given priority for protection. It is the combination of vulnerability, likelihood, and impact that should determine the priorities in designing security programs.

Crime Pattern Measurement

After the risk assessment study, it is important to monitor the patterns of ongoing problems. As noted in Chapter 1, the measurement of crime is not an easy task. Three issues are particularly important. One is the design of a useful measuring instrument, the tool for collecting essential information. It should ask about potential problems even if none has occurred at the time of the initial survey. The following categories should be covered: personnel abuses, crimes against staff, crimes against patrons, and crimes against the institution. It should be simple to use and clear. All persons using the survey should interpret it in the same way. Most good surveys avoid unnecessary items in order to keep the instrument as brief as possible. If it is difficult or not efficient to design your own survey, one can be prepared by a consultant that would include appropriate items for your particular setting. This is an easy task that should not be costly. Depending on the complexity of the situation, a site visit may not even be necessary as long as there is good communication between the administrator in charge and the specialist. Social scientists typically are trained to develop research tools for a variety of problems and can adapt these skills to research being done within the library or other public setting.

Reporting Procedure

Once an adequate survey instrument is available, the actual reporting procedure can begin. Regardless of how the data will be collected, it is important that it be done in a nonthreatening manner. Staff will cooperate in most cases when they believe that their cooperation may make the work setting better for them. Naturally, a dishonest staff member falls into another category. The reporting procedure should be routinized as part of the job description. Reference librarians may be charged with determining the amount and kinds of lost and damaged materials. Whether the librarian in charge does this or delegates the responsibility to another staff member depends on the size of the operation. In either case, the responsibility for the timely reporting should rest on the shoulders of the person reporting directly to the central collection site. All reports from the various areas of the library should be centralized. Centralization facilitates accuracy, prompt reporting, and the efficient identification of developing problems. If the work is being handled by a security officer, be sure that there is sufficient training in the handling of these kinds of data. Security personnel should also provide interim reports to the administrator in charge of the program.

The final measurement issue is the frequency of response. If time and budget permit, a monthly tabulation is advisable. It is important to be aware of developing or increasing problems before they become too serious. A monthly tabulation aids in recall as well. Naturally concerns about book theft are difficult to address with a monthly inventory. However, once the high-risk books are identified, an ongoing informal inventory can be used. If, for example, new additions are disappearing, they can be checked more frequently than the remaining sections of the collection.

Decisons regarding the implementation of security programs should be made by librarians in consultation with security personnel—not by security people alone. It is essential that the impact of any program upon the institution and its patrons and staff be considered by those professionally trained to provide library services.

Implementation

The fifth step in our model security program involves implementation. Some programs are implemented because the potential for crime has been determined. Others are initiated in reaction to actual problems.

Whether security is considered from a preventive or a reactive standpoint, it is important to consider several issues. One is cost-effectiveness. Costs must be weighed differently when personal safety as opposed to property threats is the issue. Also, the support of staff is crucial. Many otherwise strong programs have failed, not because the design was faulty or the hardware inappropriate, but because the essential staff did not do their share. Key control, book theft detection, lockup procedures, "buddy systems," crime data reporting, and others rely on support of the staff. Be sure that those involved understand exactly what is expected of them. Support is more likely to be given when the program does not complicate the work routine. During the early stages of a new program, it is important to monitor progress and delays and make necessary adjustments. It also is important to publicize new programs. In many cases, this can help to deter crime, since the library is now seen as a more secure setting, thereby increasing the risk of detection. Publicity also lets people know that the library is actively doing something to take control of problems.

It is also helpful to assess the impact of new security programs on the problems that they were designed to reduce. This can be done with the crime data that are being collected or as a separate project. If the program is working effectively, continue as designed. If not, do not hesitate to make adjustments or to seek additional advice from those vendors who installed any of the security equipment.

As we noted at the very beginning of this book, there are great difficulties involved in keeping today's libraries open and operating at full capacity. Given all the problems with securing funds, increased costs of materials, competition from television and other media, and changing information technology, we should not let the problem of crime and disruption take a greater toll than is absolutely necessary. There are problems, and serious ones, in many libraries, but there are also things that can be done to alleviate them. Providing service to the public has many rewards as well as many frustrations. Librarians, administrators, and staff, at the very least, must make a concerted effort to control crime and disruption. We cannot allow a few to destroy the benefits of our libraries for others.

NOTES

1. Louis J. Romeo, "Electronic Theft Detection Systems, Part I: Small College Libraries," *Library Security Newsletter* 2, no. 3/4 (1978): 2–18. See also: "Part

II: University Libraries," *Library and Archival Security* 3, no. 1 (1980): 1–23; "Part III: High School Libraries," *Library and Archival Security* 3, no. 2 (1980): 1–16; "Part IV: Public Libraries," *Library and Archival Security* 3 no. 3/4 (1981): 1–22; "Part V: Medical and Law Libraries," *Library and Archival Security* 3, no. 3/4 (1981): 99–114; and Nancy H. Knight, "Security Systems," in *ALA Yearbook* (Chicago: ALA, 1980, 1981, 1982).
2. Romeo, "Small College Libraries."
3. Romeo, "Public Libraries."
4. Knight, "Security Systems," 1980.
5. Ibid., 1981, 1982.
6. Pat Schindler, "The Use of Security Guards in Libraries," *Library Security Newsletter* 2 (1978): 1–6.
7. Robert Gallati, *Introduction to Private Security* (Englewood Cliffs, N.J.: Prentice-Hall, 1983).
8. "Lock and Key Control Procedures," *National School Resource Network Technical Bulletin 10,* Washington, D.C. (1976).
9. Joseph Lawler, "Theft and Mutilation in Academic Libraries: A Few Suggestions," *Rhode Island Library Bulletin* (October 1981): 17–22.
10. "Personal Safety for School Librarians," United Federation of Teachers pamphlet, cited in *Library Security Newsletter* 1 (1975): 13.

APPENDIX: LIBRARY CRIME RESEARCH PROJECT

A. Survey Questionnaire

The following letter and survey questionnaire were sent to librarians across the country.

Dear Librarian:
The Administration of Law and Justice program at the University of Lowell is sponsoring a study to determine the type and extent of crime and disruption in and against public libraries. Random samples drawn from ten states are included in this phase of the project. Our study will lead to a series of reports which will include recommendations to make libraries safer for staff and patrons. The purpose of this letter is to solicit your cooperation in the study. We simply are asking that you complete our questionnaire. There will be no further requests made and your identity will be unknown to us. Our previous studies done in fifteen states have provided social scientists and librarians with much useful information about crime patterns and prevention measures.

While we are aware that many libraries have only minor problems, it is important that we collect information from all kinds of libraries. Your library has been selected as part of your state survey. Again, let me stress that you will not be identified to us (unless you choose to do so) or anyone else. We believe strongly in the importance of this project. Your participation is a critical factor in the validity of the study and your prompt cooperation would be most welcome. Use of the self-addressed envelope will send your completed questionnaire directly to our research assistant for data processing. Should your schedule prevent full participation would you be willing to complete Page One for us? If you have any questions, then please do not hesitate to contact me.

Sincerely,

Alan Jay Lincoln, Ph.D.
Associate Professor of Law and Justice

AJL/md

(1) Which state is your library located in? _____.

(2) How would you describe the city or town in which your library is located? (Please circle one answer number)
   1. under 2,500
   2. population of 2,500–9,999
   3. population of 10,000–50,000
   4. population of 50,000–99,999
   5. population of 100,000–499,999
   6. population over 500,000

(3) Estimate the number of patrons entering your library *each day*.
   1. 1–10
   2. 11–20
   3. 21–30
   4. 31–50
   5. 51–100
   6. 101–250
   7. over 250

(4) Estimate your annual circulation. _____.

(5) Number of employees in your staff:
   A. Librarians_____
   B. Aides_____
   C. Security_____
   D. Other_____

(6) In your opinion, how much does crime and violence affect your services to the public?
   1. not at all
   2. very little
   3. moderately
   4. a great deal

(7) How would you describe the social class of the neighborhood in which your library is located?
   1. lower
   2. lower-middle
   3. middle
   4. upper-middle
   5. upper

APPENDIX A □ 165

(8) How many times during the *past 12 months* have the following occurred in your library? (Circle one answer number for each line)

		Never	Once	Twice	3–5 Times	6–10 Times	11–20 Times	+ 20 Times
A.	Intentional book damage	0	1	2	3	6	11	21
B.	Book theft	0	1	2	3	6	11	21
C.	Reference material stolen	0	1	2	3	6	11	21
D.	Equipment stolen	0	1	2	3	6	11	21
E.	Theft other than B, C, or D	0	1	2	3	6	11	21
F.	Vandalism outside the building	0	1	2	3	6	11	21
G.	Vandalism inside the building	0	1	2	3	6	11	21
H.	Vandalism of patrons' cars	0	1	2	3	6	11	21
I.	Vandalism of staff cars	0	1	2	3	6	11	21
J.	Vandalism of equipment	0	1	2	3	6	11	21
K.	Drug use by patrons/staff	0	1	2	3	6	11	21
L.	Drug sales by patrons/staff	0	1	2	3	6	11	21
M.	Verbal abuse of patrons	0	1	2	3	6	11	21
N.	Verbal abuse of staff	0	1	2	3	6	11	21
O.	Acts of "indecent exposure"	0	1	2	3	6	11	21
P.	Assault on patrons	0	1	2	3	6	11	21
Q.	Assault on staff	0	1	2	3	6	11	21
R.	Arson or suspected arson	0	1	2	3	6	11	21

(9) Have crime/disruption caused you in the last 12 months to:

		Never	Once	Twice	3–5 Times	6–10 Times	+ 10 Times
A.	Close your library	0	1	2	3	6	11
B.	Close a branch library	0	1	2	3	6	11
C.	Change your operating hours	0	1	2	3	6	11
D.	Be without operating equipment (Xerox, A.V., etc.)	0	1	2	3	6	11
E.	Stop programs for the community	0	1	2	3	6	11
F.	Call the police	0	1	2	3	6	11

(10) How close is your library to :

		Same block	Within sight	Less than .5 mile	Less than 1 mile	More than 1 mile
A.	Police station	1	2	3	4	5
B.	Elementary school (public)	1	2	3	4	5
C.	Junior high school (public)	1	2	3	4	5
D.	Senior high school (public)	1	2	3	4	5
E.	Park or playground	1	2	3	4	5

(11) Would you estimate when *most* problems have occurred:
   1. During open daylight hours
   2. During open after dark hours
   3. During closed daylight hours
   4. During closed after dark hours

(12) Estimate the percentage of your patrons that are:
   1. 18 years old and younger _____
   2. between 19 and 55 _____
   3. over 55 years old _____

(13) Estimate the total amount lost due to crime and disruption (vandalism, theft, book loss, etc.) over the last 12 months:
   0. none
   1. less than $100
   2. $101–$250
   3. $251–$500
   4. $501–$1,000
   5. $1,001–$2,500
   6. $2,501–$5,000
   7. $5,001–$10,000
   8. over $10,000

(14) The most common kind of housing in the neighborhood around your library is:
   1. housing projects/tenements
   2. apartments
   3. duplexes
   4. small single family homes
   5. large single family homes
   6. luxury apartments/condominiums
   7. not a residential area

(15) If you would be willing to distribute a short version of this survey to your staff then please put your library name and mailing address here. Only a few libraries will be selected for this followup.

   _____
   _____
   Contact person: _____

(16) Does your library have any of the following security devices or security programs? Circle one number for each line.

	No	Yes
A. Electronic intrusion detection system (motion, sound, etc.) *inside* the library	0	1

B. Closed circuit television monitors	0	1
C. Automatic communication link with police or central monitoring station in case of break-in	0	1
D. Portable emergency signaling device (wrist alarms, pocket alarms, etc.)	0	1
E. Locked room to store valuables	0	1
F. Uniformed guards or police in library	0	1
G. Plainclothes guards or police in library	0	1
H. Planned patrol coverage by local police	0	1
I. Smoke or heat detector	0	1
J. Book theft detection system	0	1

(17) How many of the outside doors and ground-level windows in your library have the following security devices? Circle one number for each line.

	None	Some	All
A. Deadbolt locks or other special security locks on outside doors	0	1	2
B. Intrusion alarms on outside doors	0	1	2
C. Security screens on ground-level windows	0	1	2
D. Unbreakable glass or plastic in outdoor ground-level windows	0	1	2

(18) What was the total amount spent on crime prevention in the last 12 months? (this includes security devices and security personnel)
   0. none
   1. less than $250
   2. $251–$500
   3. $501–$1,000
   4. $1,001–$2,500
   5. $2,501–$5,000
   6. $5,001–$10,000
   7. over $10,000

(19) If you installed security devices or hired security personnel within the last three years, then how much has crime and disruption declined?
   0. not at all
   1. 10%
   2. 20%
   3. 30%
   4. 40%
   5. 50%
   6. 60%
   7. 70%
   8. 80%
   9. 90% or more

(20) Do you carry any personal protection device while at work such as a gun, Mace, whistle, etc.?
0. NO
1. YES (what is it?_____)

(21) To the best of your knowledge, does anyone on your staff carry such a device?
0. NO
1. YES (what is it?_____)

(22) Has crime and disruption or the fear of crime caused any of the following? Circle one number for each line.

	No	Yes
A. Your asking not to work after dark	0	1
B. A staff member asking not to work after dark	0	1
C. Your being picked up after work for safety reasons	0	1
D. Escorting staff to their cars at closing	0	1
E. Staff training to handle critical situations	0	1

The following questions about the person filling out this survey are optional. But we hope you will answer them because they will help us to understand better the patterns of crime and to suggest prevention techniques:

(23) Sex: 0. Male   1. Female

(24) Age: 1. Under 25   2. 25–40   3. over 40

(25) Your position:
   1. Head librarian
   2. Other librarian
   3. Aid
   4. Security staff
   5. Other:

(26) Have you been the victim of a personal crime or crime against your property while in the library?
   0. Never
   1. Once

2. Twice
3. 3–5 times
4. 6–10 times
5. 11–20 times
6. over 20 times

Thank you for your patience and cooperation.

APPENDIX: LIBRARY CRIME RESEARCH PROJECT

B. State Data Acquisition Form

State level data are available for all 50 states at a cost of $28.50 for a complete set. The data on crime and disruption as well as patterns of security are included. Photocopy the form below for ordering purposes.

Send ( ) copy(ies) of the Library Crime Research Project State Level Data to:

Name: _____

Title/Position: _____

Address: _____

_____

City: _____ State: _____ Zip _____

Make checks payable to: A M Research Associates, Inc.
Mail to: PO Box 639, Durham, New Hampshire 03824

INDEX

Page numbers followed by the letter "t" plus a number indicate data is contained in the table on the designated page; i.e., 10t2 indicates data is to be found on page 10 in table 2. Page numbers followed by the letter "f" plus a number indicate data is contained in the figure on the designated page; i.e., 51f7 indicates data is to be found on page 51 in figure 7. Data in either tables or figures may in some cases also be found in the text on those designated pages.

Abuse of staff. See Patron behavior, harassment
Age, as crime factor, 17t7, 85, 88, 119–121
  see also Juvenile crime
Aggravated assault. See Assault
Alarm systems, 138, 139
  see also Security systems, types of
Alcohol, as problem in the library, 78, 131
American Libraries, 61
American Library Association (ALA), survey on inventory practices, 35
American Library Association Yearbook, 130
American Library Directory, 66
Arson, 9, 14t4, 15t5, 19, 25, 28, 29, 39, 59–61, 62f10, 73t14, 79, 80, 81t16, 84t17, 85t18, 95, 109, 111t27, 114t28, 115, 116t29, 118t30, 119, 121, 122t31, 125t34, 134
Assault, 9t1, 10t2, 11, 12t3, 14t4, 15t5, 16t6, 17t7, 18t8, 19, 25, 29, 31, 32, 59, 61–63, 73t14, 79, 80, 81t16, 82, 84t17, 85t18, 86t19, 87, 95, 99, 109, 111t27, 114t28, 115, 116t27, 118t30, 119, 120, 121, 122t31, 125t34, 138, 153–155

Attacks on staff, teachers. See Assault; Crimes, in schools

Behavior. See Criminal behavior; Patron behavior
Biological origins of criminal behavior, 22
Bold, Rudolph, quoted, 53–54, 55
Bomb threats, 32
Book and materials mutilation, 35–46, 73t14, 74, 81t16, 83, 84t17, 85t18, 86t19, 94, 95, 109, 110, 111t27, 113, 114t28, 115, 116t29, 118t30, 119, 121, 122t31, 123, 124t32, 125t34, 138, 151, 152f21
Book damage. See Book and materials mutilation
Book theft, 7, 25, 33–35, 37, 47–50, 73t14, 74, 75–77, 81t16, 82, 83, 84t17, 85t18, 91, 94, 95, 99, 109, 111t27, 113, 114t28, 115, 116t29, 117, 118t30, 120, 121, 122t31, 123, 124t32, 125t34, 126, 128, 129, 134–136, 138, 141
  control programs, 146–151
  see also Booknappers

173

Booknappers, 51f7
Buder, Leonard, quoted, 30–31
Budgets. *See* Cost of crime
Bureau of Justice Statistics Technical Report (March 1983), 16
Burglary, 9t1, 10t2, 12t3, 14t4, 15t5, 16t6, 27–28, 33, 138, 143, 144
Burns Security Institute study, 71, 72f12

Camera surveillance, as crime deterrent, 139, 141
Carnegie Report on Fair Practices in Higher Education, 48
Child abuse, 34
Circulation of library collection, 68–69, 82, 83
  effect on crime, 113–115
City crime rates. *See* Crime rates, urban
City size, as crime factor, 121–123, 124t33
Closed circuit television. *See* Security systems, types of
Commercial crime, 27–28
Community factors, effect on crime rate, 109–126
  see also Crime studies
Computer theft, 76f13
Conklin, John, 89
  quoted, 90
Cost of crime, 1, 28, 89, 90, 91–105, 112, 117, 128, 131, 133
  direct, 91–97
  indirect, 97–105
  see also Crime prevention, programs
Crime, defining, 19–21
Crime detection systems. *See* Crime prevention
Crime index, 9
Crime patterns, 5, 8–18, 71–80, 86–87, 89, 94, 99, 100–102, 130–136
  measurement of, 158–159
  see also Crime studies; Library crime

Crime prevention, 32, 33, 127–160
  costs, 97–105, 120, 121
  designing programs, 155–160
  implementing programs, 160
  low-cost programs, 143–155
  programs, 136–155
  security systems, 30, 62, 89, 90, 95, 112, 119, 123, 127–160
  see also Book and materials mutilation; Book theft
Crime rates, 8, 9t1, 10t2, 11–16, 17t7, 18t8
  increasing, 1, 11
  rural, suburban, 1, 11, 29
  urban, 1, 11, 29
  see also Crime studies; Library crime; Library Crime Research Project
Crime records, 7–8
  see also *Uniform Crime Reports (U.C.R.)*
Crime statistics, 5
  see also Crime patterns; Crime studies; Library Crime Research Project; *Uniform Crime Reports (U.C.R.)*
Crime studies, 27–63
Crime theory, 21
Crimes
  causes of, 21–26
  costs of, 1, 28, 89, 90, 91–105
  in buildings, 1
  in commercial buildings, 27–28
  in private settings, 1
  in public places, 2–3, 11
  in public transportation, 31–32
  in recreational areas, 32–33
  in religious buildings, 30–31
  in schools, 29–30
  measuring, 4–8
  reporting, 29
  types of, 8, 9t1, 10, 11
  see also Crime studies; Juvenile crime; Library crime
Criminal behavior, 19–26
  see also Crime studies; Measuring crime

Criminal justice system, 8, 90
    see also Crime studies; Crimes
Criminologists. See Impact of crime
Culp, Robert, quoted, 47
Cultural factors, and criminal behavior, 24

Defensible acts, 19–20
Delinquency, 21
    see also Juvenile crime
Delph, Edward, 50
    quoted, 51
Deviant behavior. See Patron behavior
Differential association, 24
Disruption in the library, 2
    see also Patron behavior; Vandalism
Disruptive behavior. See Patron behavior
Documents, mutilation of, 46f5
Dogs, as property protectors, 137
Drop-in programs. See Police patrols
Drug use, violations, 9, 25, 33, 55, 73t14, 77, 80, 81t16, 82, 83, 84t17, 85t18, 109, 111t27, 113, 114t28, 115, 116t29, 118t30, 120, 122t31, 125t34

Elderly, as crime victims, 18
Electronic security systems. See Security systems, types of
Embezzlement, 14t4
Emerson, William L., quoted, 42
Entry points, protection of, 137–138
Equipment, damage to. See Vandalism
Equipment theft. See Larceny-theft; Vandalism

False alarms, 129
Fear of crime. See Impact of crime
Federal Bureau of Investigation (F.B.I.), 5, 59
Felony, 19
Forgery/counterfeiting, 14t4, 25
Fraud, 14t4

Gallati, Robert, 142, 143
Genetic link to crime, 22
Geographical region, as crime factor, 11, 29, 83–85, 92, 99, 102
Gouke, Mary, quoted, 39, 42

Harassment of staff. See Patron behavior
Haskell, Martin R., 21
Hendrick, Clyde, 36, 37, 40, 42
High-risk crime areas, 28, 30, 62, 80–82, 100, 102–105
Hijackings, 32, 39
Hillery, George, 33
Hooton, Earnest, 22
Hoppe, Ronald, 43
    quoted, 40, 44
Household crimes, 16t6, 28

Impact of crime, 88–108, 111–112, 114–115, 116–117
    on victims, 18
Incidence of crime. See Crime patterns
Indecent exposure, 73t14, 78, 80, 81t16, 83, 84t17, 85t18, 109, 111t27, 114t28, 116t29, 118t30, 120, 121, 122t31, 125t34
Individual as criminal, emphasis on, 22–24
Interiors, protection of, 138–141
Inventory, as theft deterrent, 34–35, 147

"Jock the Ripper," book mutilator, 41f2
Justice, Department of, 5
Juvenile crime, 7, 8, 9, 11, 14t4, 15, 16, 17t7, 25–26, 60, 61, 119–121, 130–134
    see also individual crimes

Kaske, Neal K., quoted, 48
Kennedy, John, 60, 61

Knight, Nancy H., quoted, 130
Kurth, William, 49

Larceny-theft, 9t1, 10t2, 11, 12t3, 14t4, 15t5, 17t7, 18t8, 27, 30, 32, 33, 82, 83t17, 84t18, 111t27, 114t28, 116t29, 118t30, 120, 121, 122t31, 125t34, 130, 134, 135, 141
    control programs, 146–151
Law enforcement agencies, 1, 20
    and library crime, 29, 117, 121
Lawler, Joseph, 151
Library and Archival Security, 38, 128
Library crime, 33–63
    acceptance of, 34
    costs of, 89–105
    dealing with serious crimes, 130–136
    effect on services, 92–97, 112, 115, 117
    factors affecting crime rate, 109–126
    fear of, 93
    high-risk areas, 30, 62, 80–82, 98, 100, 102–105
    informing police, 29, 117, 121
    low-risk areas, 82–83, 100
    recording data, 29
    reporting, 29, 73t14, 78, 81t16, 95t22, 96–97, 115, 159
    research project, 66–87
    see also Patron behavior; *also individual crimes*
Library Crime Research Project, 66–87
    crime patterns, 71–80
    data acquisition form, 171
    high-crime libraries, 80–82, 91, 92
    low-crime libraries, 82–83
    number participating in, 67
    patron behavior, 66–71
    questionnaire, 67, 71, 163–169
    sample, 66–71
    survey instrument, 67
    types of crimes surveyed, 71–80
    see also Crime prevention

Library factors, effect on crime rate, 109–126
Library losses due to crime. *See* Cost of crime
Library security. *See* Crime prevention
Library security checklist, 156–158
Library services, effects of crime on, 92–97, 112, 115, 117
Library staff
    abuse by patrons, 54, 73t14, 77–78, 80, 81t16, 82, 83, 84t17, 85t18, 86t19, 87, 99, 109, 111t27, 114t28, 115, 116t29, 118t30, 122t31, 124t32, 125t34, 126
    burnout, 54–55
    morale, 149–150
    screening, 149–150
    security measures by, 105–108
    size of, 69, 83, 117–119
    victimization, 105–108, 109
    wage equity, 150
    see also Assault; Crime prevention, programs; Impact of crime; Library Crime Research Project; Patron behavior
Lighting, as crime deterrent, 137
Lincoln, Alan, 33
Locks, as crime deterrent, 137–138
    see also Security systems, types of
Loitering, 131
Lombroso, Cesare, theory of, 22
Low-cost security programs, 143–155
Low-risk crime areas, 82–83, 100, 103

Manslaughter, 9t1, 10t2, 12t3, 14t4, 15t5
Massachusetts/New Hampshire library study, 86–87
Measuring crime, 4–8, 158–159
Mentally disturbed people in library, 51–54, 79
Microfilm, as deterrent to book mutilation, 46
Midwest, crime in. *See* Geographical region, as crime factor

Mirrors, as crime deterrent, 144, 145
Misdemeanor, 19
Modeling. See "Modeling effect"
"Modeling effect," influence on crimes, 39, 42
Motion detection systems, 139
Motor vehicle theft, 9t1, 10t2, 11, 12t3, 14t4, 15t5, 16t6, 25, 28
Movement controls in library, 147–149
Munn, Ralph, quoted, 34, 38, 47
Murder, 9t1, 10t2, 11, 14t4, 15t5, 19, 33, 61
Murfin, Marjorie, 36, 37, 40, 42
  quoted, 39, 42
Mutilation of books. See Book and materials mutilation
Mutilation/theft in British universities, 42, 48

Narcissism, 23
Neighborhood characteristics, as crime factor, 70–71
Neutralization, techniques of, 25
Niland, Powell, 49
Nonviolent crime. See Crimes, types of
Northeast, crime in. See Geographical region, as crime factor
Nutrition and criminal behavior, 22

Obscene phone calls, 54
Offender surveys. See Surveys, offender

Paris, Janelle, 50
Patron age. See Age, as crime factor
Patron behavior, 1, 7, 19, 50–63, 77–79, 109, 152–153
  dealing with, 130–134
  disturbed, 51–54
  harassment, 54, 73t14, 77–78, 80, 81t16, 82, 83, 84t17, 85t18, 86t19, 87, 99, 111t27, 114t28, 116t29, 118t30, 120, 122t31, 124t32, 125t34

influencing factors, 45, 46
  role in crimes, 43–44
  sexual, 51, 131, 144
  see also Crime prevention, programs
Patron population, as crime factor, 115–117
Patrons, library
  perceptions of library, 1
  see also Patron behavior
Peer pressure, 25–26
Periodicals, mutilation of. See Book and materials mutilation
Personality disorders and criminal behavior, 23
Physical type theory of criminal behavior, 22
Pocket picking, 17t7, 18t8, 27
Police
  intervention in library crime, 91, 96–97, 100
  location of, 123–125
  patrols, 127, 132–133, 145–146
  see also Crime prevention; Library crime, reporting
Population, as crime factor, 8, 9, 11, 12t3, 68, 82–83, 100, 115, 122
Post traumatic stress disorder, as determinant of behavior, 23
Premenstrual tension (PMT), as determinant of behavior, 23
Problem patrons. See Patron behavior
Property crime, 9t1, 10t2, 11, 12t3, 15t5, 29
Property lines. See Property protection
Property protection, 136–143
Prosecution policies, library, 146
Prostitution, 9
Protecting the library. See Crime prevention
Psychoanalytic theories of criminal behavior, 23
Psychopathic behavior, 23
Public places
  access to, 2–3
  crimes in, 2–3
  definition of, 2–3

Public transportation, crime in, 31–32
Purse snatching, 17t7, 18t8, 25

Racial attacks, 30
Rape, 9t1, 10t2, 11, 12t3, 14t4, 15t5, 16t6, 17t7, 18t8, 33
Recording systems, crime, 29
Recreational areas, crime in, 32–33
Reference material, theft of. See Theft, reference materials
Regional patterns. See Geographical region, as crime factor
Religious institutions, crime in, 30–31, 61
Reporting crime, 159
  see also Crime patterns
Risk assessment study, 158
Risk-taking behavior, 26
Robbery, 9t1, 10t2, 11, 12t3, 14t4, 15t5, 16t6, 17t7, 18t8, 27–28, 138
Roberts, Matt, 50
Romeo, Louis, 128
  quoted, 129
Rural crime rates. See Crime rates, rural, suburban

Schindler, Pat, 141–142
Schools
  crime in, 2–3, 6, 29–30
  location of, as crime factor, 123, 124t32
  security programs in, 143–144
Security. See Crime prevention
Security checklist for the library, 156–158
Security guards, use of in libraries, 62, 69, 70, 97, 101–102, 117, 118, 119, 127, 137, 139, 141–143
Security measures, in the library. See Crime prevention
Security systems, types of, 32, 99–105, 127–160
Sex, as crime factor, 15t5, 18t8, 86, 88

Sexual assault, 31
  see also Patron behavior; Rape
Sheldon, William, 22
Shoplifting, 27
Simmel, Edward, 40, 43
  quoted, 44
Simple assault. See Assault
Situational factors, in book mutilation, 42, 43, 45, 46
Size of library, as crime factor, 9, 68, 69, 71, 82–83, 113, 115–117
  see also Library staff, size of
Smoke detectors. See Security systems, types of
Social deviance, 20
Social structural disorganization, 24
Society/group as criminal, emphasis on, 24–26
Socioeconomic class and crime, 49, 82, 125–126
Souter, G. H., quoted, 37, 48, 50
South, crime in. See Geographical region, as crime factor
Special libraries, arson in, 59–60
Spouse abuse, 34
States, and library crime
  crime patterns in, 110–112
  highest crime rates in, 111
  lowest crime rates in, 110–111
Stolen property, possession of, 14t4
"Streaking," 55, 59
Suburban crime rates. See Crime rates, rural, suburban
Surveys
  crime pattern measurement, 158–159
  Library Crime Research Project, 66–87, 127–128, 163–171
  of serious library crime, 130–136
  offender, 6–7
  risk assessment study, 158
  security checklist, 156–158
  security system users, 128–130
  victimization, 5–6, 15, 16t6, 18t8
  see also Impact of crime
Sutherland, Edwin, 24

Tappan, Paul, quoted, 19
Television surveillance, as crime deterrent, 139, 140f17
Theft
fear of, 77
reference materials, 75, 76, 80, 81t16, 82, 83, 84t17, 85t18, 109, 110, 111t27, 113, 114t28, 115, 116t29, 118t30, 119, 120, 121, 122t32, 123, 124t32
see also Book theft; Larceny-theft
Theft detection systems. See Security systems, types of
Theories of criminal behavior, 22-23, 88
Traffic patterns, patron, 148
Trends in crime. See Crime patterns

Uniform Crime Reports (U.C.R.), 5, 6, 9, 15, 16, 28, 83, 111

Vandalism, 6, 9, 14t4, 15, 25, 29, 30, 31, 33, 55, 59, 62f10, 71-72, 73t14, 74-75, 80, 81t16, 82, 83, 84t17, 85t18, 86t19, 87, 91, 94f15, 95, 96, 99, 109, 110, 111t27, 114t28, 115, 116t29, 119, 121, 122t31, 123, 125t34, 130, 134, 135, 138, 155
see also Book and materials mutilation
Verbal abuse of staff. See Patron behavior, harassment
Victimization, personal, 85-86, 105-108

Victimization surveys. See Surveys, victimization
Victimology, 88-89
Vietnam syndrome. See Post traumatic stress disorder
Vinnes, Norman, 49
Violent crime, 9t1, 10t2, 11, 12t3, 14t4, 15t5, 16t6, 30, 31, 33, 79, 94, 122, 142f18, 155
see also individual crimes
Violent School-Safe School Report to Congress, 29
Visibility enhancement, as crime deterrent, 144-145
Vocino, Michael, 52
quoted, 53
Vogel, Betty, quoted, 52, 54

Ward, Colin, quoted, 35-36
Warning systems. See Security systems, types of
Weapons, possession of, 14t4, 17t7, 18t8
Weiss, Dana, 42
quoted, 36, 37
West, crime in. See Geographical region, as crime factor

XYY chromosome pattern, and crime, 22

Yablonsky, Lewis, 21

Zimmerman, Lee, quoted, 42

DATE DUE